Democratic Audit of Poland 2014

WARSAW STUDIES IN POLITICS AND SOCIETY

Edited by
Radosław Markowski

VOLUME 2

PETER LANG
EDITION

Radosław Markowski / Michał Kotnarowski /
Michał Wenzel / Marta Żerkowska-Balas

Democratic Audit of Poland 2014

PETER LANG
EDITION

Bibliographic Information published by the Deutsche Nationalbibliothek
The Deutsche Nationalbibliothek lists this publication in the Deutsche Nationalbibliografie; detailed bibliographic data is available in the internet at http://dnb.d-nb.de.

This publication was financially supported
by the Center for the Study of Democracy and
the University of Social Sciences and Humanities Warsaw.

ISSN 2193-3774
ISBN 978-3-631-65691-4 (Print)
E-ISBN 978-3-653-05061-5 (E-Book)
DOI 10.3726/978-3-653-05061-5

Peter Lang Edition is an Imprint of Peter Lang GmbH.

Peter Lang – Frankfurt am Main · Bern · Bruxelles · New York ·
Oxford · Warszawa · Wien

This publication has been peer reviewed.

www.peterlang.com

Table of Contents

Introduction

Democratic audits in the world have an established, if not a very long tradition. They were created not so much as scientific studies, but rather as *policy analysis* covering the issues of macro-democracy both in its normative visions and in its performance, including practical diagnosis of its dysfunctions.

Particular national traditions of audits differ greatly; in some the performance of democracy is assessed in details, while in others it is evaluated rather generally. Some believe that the quality of democracy cannot be discussed without precisely defining what model of democracy is assumed, while others ignore this issue altogether. Some models were created when concerned citizens and social science professionals noticed grave deficiencies in the functioning of democracy, or were concerned about its future, while others were the outcome of scholarly reflection. Most are the practical consequence of the belief that a collective and public discussion of issues concerning political order is a necessary condition for its success.

The best known and at the same time chronologically the first was the Democratic Audit of the United Kingdom[1]. Its first edition was released at the beginning of the 1990s. The authors of the document reflect on its essence in the following words: "a democratic audit or an analytical democracy assessment, as it is also known, is a comprehensive and systematic assessment of a country's political life from the viewpoint of the key principles such as citizen control over the decision-making process and political equality in the exercise of that control."

It is therefore a sort of a test of the "health" of a country's democracy. Almost the same might be said about the general idea and the chief aim of this publication, the first Democratic Audit of Poland (DAP). However, due to the fact that this is the first edition of a planned series, it is characterized by some particularities described later.

The Australian Democracy Audit is, on the other hand, more "interactive" and publication-oriented, being released both in the form of books

1 http://democracy-uk-2012.democraticaudit.com

and magazine articles. It is also reactive, as it concurrently addresses legislation changes or current political decisions.

Reflection on the quality of democracy in the Netherlands has a long and complex history, but the Dutch audit truly gained in speed in 2002, when the political shooting star Pim Fortuyn revolutionized the Dutch political scene and was murdered soon afterwards. His death resulted in the conclusion made both by politicians of that country and academics that the performance of the Dutch democracy is far from ideal. Therefore, they decided to initiate a reflection over the state of the Dutch democracy as one of the tools to improve its condition.

These examples of three democracy audits and their genesis aim at pointing at the diverse reasons for their creation. Our motivations to start a democratic audit in Poland are closest to the British case.

Currently, in many countries democracy audits significantly contribute to citizens' self-reflection, and publicizing their findings becomes a media event. For some time now, appreciating the importance of those projects, the Stockholm Institute IDEA has decided to coordinate those dispersed projects of particular countries, with the aim to encourage some comparability. The methodological assistance is of great significance and the IDEA Institute offers it to the teams in need.

At the same time, let us note that, together with the global spread of democracy as a system of governance and with the increasing quest for democracy, a range of institutions systematically dealing with its quality assessments emerged, alongside such long-standing projects as Freedom House or Polity. For instance, there are interesting initiatives by the Bertelsmann Foundation, such as Bertelsmann Transformation Index (BTI) or Sustainable Governance Indicators (SGI). They focus on numerous aspects of democracy, the state and the market economy relevant in democratizing countries, i.e. on the attributes we do not usually analyse in traditional stable democracies of Western Europe and the Anglo-Saxon world. Another new and interesting initiative is the World Justice Forum, which publishes systematic global assessment of the state performance, known as *Rule of Law Index*. It assesses selected aspects of the operation of the state and the law, elections, as well as the fundamental civil and political rights. In 2012, an extremely important project complementary towards the previous ones was initiated and named *Varieties of Democracy (VoD)*. After many years of criticism of the abovementioned initiatives for assuming a "linear", or one dimensional, model of democracy, a study of various types and models of democracy was launched.

Finally, in this necessarily short description of national traditions of "democracy audits" it must be stressed that these projects are comparative in substance, but comparative in terms of time rather than space. New initiatives and actions of IDEA will be moving towards comparability of these projects on the international level. We believe these activities to be timely and necessary, even though we also think that such projects should always be nationally specific. In other words, they should be case studies instead of classic comparative studies. The current edition of the Democratic Audit of Poland (DAP) is the first one and, in our intention, a "pilot" study, since it also tests the limits of availability of relevant data on Polish institutions for scientists and experts willing to evaluate the state of democracy in contemporary Poland. It brings innovative approach to the interpretation of both existing data and mass studies of the Polish society. Last but not least, this DAP is a "pilot" edition since it covers quite a wide range of issues. We realise that not all aspects we cover are considered by theories of democracy as its constitutive elements. Public administration is an example of such a borderline sphere, even though among well-known academics we find those willing to consider, as they themselves call it, "effective bureaucracy" as one of the five spheres of democracy (Linz, Stepan 1996).

In order to defend the broad approach to the assessment of the Polish democracy, we should reiterate that in the first pilot version of our audit we wanted to look at democracy itself, as well as the phenomena and spheres of life directly connected with it, from as broad a perspective as possible. We call it a "pilot" study because we are open for a discussion and encourage critical evaluation of our conclusions. The subsequent versions of this document: DAP 2016, DAP 2018 and so on will undoubtedly be more limited, but at the same time more standardised. Ultimately, the Democratic Audit of Poland is envisaged as a longitudinal project. It will be a repeated analysis of the state of Polish democracy in subsequent years.

We will be paying special attention to the dynamics of changes of particular aspects of democracy. Not only as academics and experts, but also as engaged citizens would we like to live to the day when we could put our activity on hold while claiming that in this political system there is no more room for improvement. We remain, however, realistic and know that democracy is characterised by immanent contradictions; hence, crises are its essence. Therefore, we should brace ourselves for long years of analyses and recommendations. We consider it important for the reports submitted every second year to constitute a significant reference point and guidance for decision-makers on what to do, how to improve the law, how to change our politics and politicians, as well as how to encourage citizens to act for the democratic public good.

We wish to conclude with a few methodological remarks. The data used in this report are, in most cases, publically available. There are "objective" data from such sources as GUS (Central Statistical Office), ministry offices, etc. (first pillar), as well as the data from public opinion surveys (second pillar). The third pillar of our audit is the so-called "expert survey," which is complementary to the public data. Our experts were selected according to meritocratic criteria on the basis of their commonly recognised competences in the selected areas of public life. We generally treat the collective results of their assessment as "para-objective" descriptions of the Polish democratic reality. It often occurs that expert opinions do not fully coincide with the statistical data, and the latter are occasionally quite contrary to the citizens' assessment. Let's emphasize it clearly at this point: this audit does not aim at resolving these allegedly conflicting messages, as our DAP is not a classical scientific inquiry. We are aware that professional perception of reality often differs from the assessment of a given phenomenon or problem seen through the eyes of citizens who are non-professionals. This report is meant to demonstrate these discrepancies. However, it is not supposed to determine which party is right.

For instance, the data of PGSW[2] shows that as many as 2/3 of the electorate of the major opposition party in 2010 claimed that in 2009 Poland was not the so-called "green island" and did not consider the objective indicator of the Polish GDP growth of 1.7% in that year. The statistical data

2 PGSW – Polish National Electoral Study; the quoted result was described in more detail in: Tworzecki, Hubert and Radosław Markowski, "Knowledge and Partisan Bias: An Uneasy Relationship," East European Politics and Societies (EEPS), Vol. 28, No. 4 (Nov. 2014), pp. 836-862.

on this issue, both Polish and foreign, differ only as to the amount of the growth, namely whether it was 1.6% or 1.7%. Let this serve as an example of the dilemmas we faced while writing this report. This result might be interpreted in two ways: the pessimistic conclusion that great numbers of Poles are unable to objectively assess the reality they live in; or a positive one, suggesting that we are dealing with strong ties between citizens forming a particular electorate and the party representing them. A successful party message for the electorate is important especially in the times of low party prestige, and the alleged lack of their socialisation and mobilisation skills. Similar discrepancies might occur between the objective data and opinions of average Poles or experts. Such discrepancies constitute an immanent part of democracy. We should be aware of them.

In the report we analyse ten areas of democracy that comprise a large number of more detailed aspects. Among them we distinguish such fundamental issues for democracy as the rule of law, the party system, as well as political accountability. There are also less fundamental issues, including the assessment of public administration. The order of chapters is not accidental; we start with the fundamental issues, namely the political community and the rule of law. We finish with feedback mechanisms, namely elite accountability and responsiveness. Chapter six describes and analyzes Poles' attitudes towards democracy, their opinions, positions, and values related to democracy. It differs from the others, as it constitutes a description and evaluation of Poles as democratic citizens.

At the end, we ought to emphasize that this first edition of the Democratic Audit of Poland covers a wider range of analytical areas than our target comparative project, whose goal will be a dynamic evaluation assessing whether in a given area the state of Polish democracy is improving or worsening. That is why in DAP 2014 we used several international comparative studies and comparisons, some of them dating back many years. We stress the significance of other similar initiatives that, while using different methodology, are oriented at both inter-country comparisons and at changes occurring in time, such as *Bertelsmann Transformation Index* (BTI). An overview of BTI Reports plus our DAP will undoubtedly give the reader a more complete picture of the state of Polish democracy.

Finally, this project owes its existence to *Polish Confederation Lewiatan*, in particular to its president Henryka Bochniarz and its executive director

Lech Pilawski. We would like to emphasize that this project would have not been possible without the substantial generous funds from *Lewiatan,* as well as an important supplementary contribution from *Academy for the Development of Philanthropy in Poland* and *Polish-American Freedom Foundation.* Analyses and studies contained in this volume were possible thanks to the grant no. NN116533740 Polish National Election Study 2011, awarded by the National Science Centre (Poland). The Principal Investigator for this project was professor Radosław Markowski. The survey was conducted by Public Opinion Research Centre (CBOS) in Warsaw in cooperation with the Institute of Political Studies of the Polish Academy of Sciences, based on partnership agreement. In chapters 1, 7 and 8 data from earlier editions of Polish National Election Study are used. They were financed by the State Committee for Scientific Research.

Last but not least, we would like to thank our numerous experts, reviewers and the DAP Academic Board members (Bogdan Mach, Mirosława Grabowska, Tomasz Schimanek and Jacek Wasilewski) for their plentiful remarks, friendly criticism and proposals for improvement. We would also like to thank Krzysztof Iszkowski and Borys Markowski for their contribution in data gathering and analyses.

1. Political community

For democracy it is important that the state respects the rights of all, including individuals who are not citizens of that state, as well as individuals who are its citizens, but belong to minority groups. This chapter is dedicated to this issue. Its first part concerns the rights of non-citizens. In accordance with international conventions, a resident individual of foreign citizenship should have fundamental political rights safeguarded. We analyze, among others, their possibility of participating in elections as well as entering into associations. As a context crucial for these rights we also present the situation of these individuals on the labour market.

An important related issue is the protection of refugees. We are interested in legal mechanisms related to protection of refugees as well as assessment of their integration process in Poland. At the end we analyze the process of acquiring Polish citizenship by foreign nationals. An ideal model of democracy provides the possibility to acquire citizenship for individuals who have settled down in a given country and bind their future with it.

In the second part of this chapter we focus on the rights of citizens belonging to minority groups. First, we present legal mechanisms protecting them from exclusion. Then we outline the results of an empirical analysis of effectiveness of their representation.

1.1 Ensuring the rights of individuals who are not citizens of the Republic of Poland

1.1.1 Political participation of foreigners

In accordance with the Polish law, political rights of foreign nationals are relatively limited. The right to vote and be elected in national elections is granted only to citizens of Poland. Since 1st May 2004, the right to vote and to be elected in regional elections has also been provided for citizens of EU member states remaining permanently in a given constituency. Non-EU citizens have no voting rights. Foreign nationals may join associations (if their statute permits) but these associations can be established only by individuals permanently residing in Poland.

Poland has not ratified the European Convention on participation of foreign nationals in public life on the local level. Article 6 of this document gives every foreigner living in a given country for at least 5 years the right to participate in elections as well as the right to stand for office in local elections (Council of Europe – ETS no. 144 – *Convention on the Participation of Foreigners in Public Life at Local Level)*. Moreover, article 5 of the convention places an obligation on the authorities to remove barriers for establishing advisory bodies, that is bodies which facilitate discussion and formulating opinions, wishes, and concerns of foreign citizens (...) in the domains which especially concern them in relation to the local public life (Kaźmierczak and Seges-Frelak 2013, p. 16).

The absence of political rights for foreigners influenced the results of the latest edition of Migrant Integration Policy Index published in 2010 (Huddleston and Niessen 2011). This report monitors the situation of migrants in selected countries in the world. The aspect that was assessed worst in relation to the situation of migrants in Poland in 2010 was the possibility of their political participation. Poland received, in this aspect, only 14 out of 100 potential points and took last but one place in the ranking of 36 states (ahead of Romania). Since the publication of Migrant Integration Policy Index, access to political rights of foreigners in Poland has not changed.

1.1.2 Situation of foreign citizens on the labour market

The latest changes in the law regulating possibilities of employment by foreign nationals have been assessed positively (Bieniecki and others 2010). In 2007, the necessity to apply for a work permit by citizens of all EU member states was abolished. Moreover, in 2008 access to the labour market for non-EU residents was eased. Additional facilitation is connected with the introduction in 2007 of *the Polish Card*, which authorizes foreign owners of the card to work in similar conditions to those of the citizens of Poland.

A great achievement of the Polish state in the field of foreigners' integration is adoption by the Council of Ministers in 2012 of a document entitled Migration Policy in Poland – current state and proposed action plan *(Migration Policy in Poland-current state and proposed action plan*). It is a document defining the objectives of migration policy of Poland and comprehensively discussing all areas of migration policy (Pawlak 2013). What is important, this program has been prepared far away from political disputes with significant participation of representatives of NGOs dealing with the issue of immigration and representatives of the academic world.

1.1.3 Granting protection to refugees

Polish legislation on providing protection for foreigners on the territory of the Republic of Poland follows Art.1A of the Geneva Convention from 1951. In accordance with these provisions, a refugee is a person who, owing to a well-founded fear of being persecuted, has left their country of origin and is unable or unwilling to avail themselves of the protection of that country (*Convention and Protocol Relating to the Status of Refugees*).

Any person granted refugee status is given the right of residence in Poland. Moreover, such a person receives, on the same basis as a Polish citizen, among others: the right to work, to run a business, the right to social security benefits, to health insurance, and the right to education in all types of schools.

During the course of the procedure on granting refugee status, an applicant may stay in an open accommodation centre. Available research did not indicate serious problems connected with the conditions in those centres (*Participatory Assessment 2010 Report. Being a refugee. How refugees and asylum-seekers experience life in Central Europe*, 2011). In extraordinary cases an applicant may be placed in a closed detention centre. Individuals who applied in Poland for refugee status but later left for another country where they were arrested are detained in those centres.

Independent studies on detention centers indicate excessive frequency of placement of applicants in these facilities. They are placed there even when not meeting certain conditions, i.e. not posing threat to the national security or public order (*Migracja to nie zbrodnia. Raport z monitoringu strzeżonych ośrodków dla cudzoziemców* [Migration Is Not a Crime. A Report on monitoring of guarded centres for foreigners], 2012, p. 39). Applicants who want to lodge an appeal against the court decision must face long delays in examination of an appeal. Another problem related to functioning of detention centres is the regime modelled on the prison system, even though most persons who are kept there committed administrative, not criminal offences. Experts note the oppressive character of detention centres *(Migration ...* p. 39).

People who have been granted refugee status are subject to Individual Integration Program. Generally speaking, this program is assessed positively; however, according to applicants participating in the program, it does not last long enough. They are unable to learn the Polish language at a level enabling communication, neither can they gain qualifications required on the labour market (*Participatory Assessment 2010 Report. Being a refugee. How refugees and asylum-seekers experience life in Central Europe*, 2011).

An important issue connected with applying for a refugee status is the functioning of offices responsible for contacts with foreigners. The results of this study indicate some improvement in performance of the regional Departments for Foreigners (Frelak and Korolec 2009; Szymańska-Matusiewicz 2012).

The general approach of the public opinion towards foreigners is positive; however, there have been negative reactions of Poles towards proposals of setting up new reception centres in their direct neighborhoods (*A ECRI Report On Poland. The fourth monitoring cycle*, 2010).

In conclusion, Polish legislation in terms of protection of refugees can be assessed positively. The main provisions of the Geneva Convention, as well as agreements within the European Union have been implemented. Implementation of the legal provisions has been taking place rather smoothly.

The state of open accommodation centres for foreigners has improved; so have the regional Departments for Foreigners. In case of closed detention centres, criticism is levelled at excessive frequency of placement in these facilities and their restrictive character.

1.1.4 Acquisition of Polish citizenship

The condition for obtaining political rights is acquisition of Polish citizenship. It is regulated by the bill on Polish citizenship (*Ustawa o obywatelstwie polskim*), which entered into law in 2012. This law introduced a range of changes adjusting Polish legislation to the requirements of the European Convention on Citizenship.

A significant change in the new law is connected with the fact that, for those born within the territory of the Republic of Poland, in order to be able to acquire citizenship, it is enough for one parent to be a citizen of Poland (in the previous wording of the law both parents had to have Polish citizenship). In case of having citizenship granted by the President of the Republic of Poland the applicant for citizenship does not need to meet any conditions.

Especially important changes connected with the new bill are related to the procedure of recognizing citizenship administratively by the regional administration. According to the existing bill, any foreign resident who has remained within the territory of Poland for a specific time (the bill defines various groups) is entitled to apply for citizenship. In the new bill the requirement for the person applying for Polish citizenship to renounce their existing citizenship has been lifted.

In case of a negative decision of the regional administration, an applicant may appeal. A new mechanism in the existing law is a requirement of Polish language competence. Changes in legislation related to recognition of citizenship are interpreted as "turning away from the vision of citizenship as a specific privilege towards a more practical concept of citizenship as a right which might be claimed in court" (*An analysis of changes concerning the rules for acquisition of Polish citizenship)*. This bill also regulates recognition of citizenship in case when a foreigner is married to a Polish citizen.

The existing legislation related to acquisition of Polish citizenship, especially recently introduced changes, should be assessed positively. These changes are a manifestation of the legal adjustment to the changing social circumstances.

1.1.5 Ensuring foreign citizens' rights – expert opinions

DAP experts positively assess regulations of situations of individuals legally residing in Poland but not being its citizens. Their status raises no doubts in terms of democratic standards. Respecting human rights of foreigners residing in Poland illegally has been assessed slightly worse but still positively (which is reflected in the value above 5).

Fig./Tab. 1.1: Protection of rights of foreign citizens

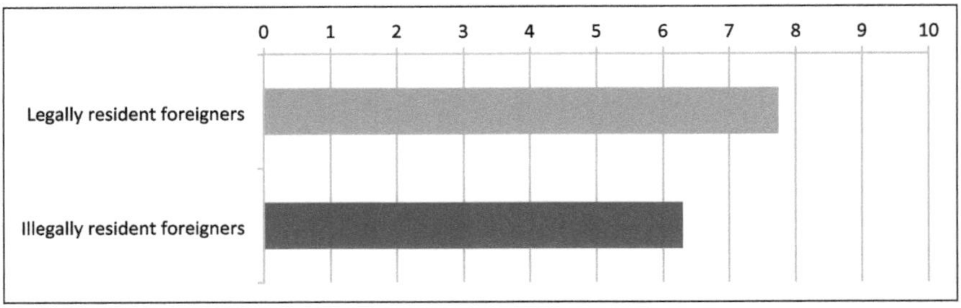

Source: DAP expert survey. Average on a scale from 0 to 10

A significant achievement of the Polish state in the field of the integration of foreigners is adoption by the Council of Ministers in 2012 of a document entitled Migration Policy in Poland-current state and proposed action plan *(Migration Policy in Poland-current state and proposed action plan*). It is a document defining the objectives of migration policy of Poland and comprehensively discussing all areas (Pawlak 2013).

1.2 Ensuring civil rights of minority groups

In this part, first we describe legal regulations protecting minority groups from exclusion. Afterwards we discuss how minority rights are actually represented in Poland.

1.2.1 Legal provisions protecting from exclusion

Legislation regarding national and ethnic minorities is contained in a number of bills. These provisions, however, concern citizens only[3].

Constitution of the Republic of Poland guarantees Polish citizens belonging to national and ethnic minority groups the freedom to maintain and develop their own language and culture, to maintain customs and traditions, the right to establish their own educational and cultural institutions and institutions designed to protect their religious identity (Art.35 of the Constitution of the Republic of Poland).

3 An overview following http://mniejszosci.narodowe.mac.gov.pl/mne/prawo/zapisy-z-konstytucji-r/6481,Podstawowe-prawa.html.

Minority rights are also regulated by international law, including the European Convention on Human Rights of November 4th 1950 and the International Convention on the Elimination of All Forms of Racial Discrimination of March 7th 1966. Moreover, Poland entered into a number of bilateral treaties, which regulate the issue of minorities in relation to immigrants from neighbouring countries.

In the opinion of DAP experts, Polish law ensures equal political rights for all citizens of Poland. The average on an 11-point scale, where 0 means a lack of equality, and 10 complete equality, is 8.85, which is very high. Among the experts there is a far-reaching consensus.

Experts who note lack of complete equality of political rights listed the groups that, in their opinion, are deprived of full rights. Most frequently, they mentioned the disabled, as many of them, despite changing the law, have no real ability to cast votes. Individual experts speak of various groups, which have formal, but not real, ability to use their voting rights, e.g. migrants.

According to experts, both national, ethnic and linguistic minorities living in the territory of Poland and religious minorities and atheists have full political rights. Experts perceive the rights of sexual minorities on a similar, i.e. positive note. Protection of political rights of these three groups raises little doubt, which is reflected in the average assessment above 8.

Fig./Tab. 1.2: Protection of political rights of minorities

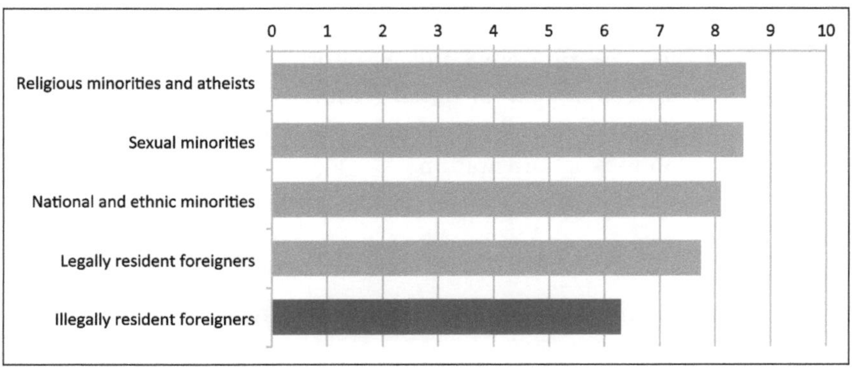

Source: DAP expert survey. Average on a scale from 0 to 10

In conclusion, civil rights of minorities, specifically regulated by national and international acts, seem to be secured. Special provisions in the regulations (for instance lifting the electoral threshold for minority electoral lists) seem to be reasonable. However, some analysts note the failure to consider minorities in different regulations than dedicated bills (Szulecka 2013).

1.2.2 Implementation of legal mechanisms of respecting the rights of minorities

In spite of the fact that anti-discrimination regulations have a relatively long tradition, implementation of the principle of equal treatment encounters numerous barriers.

Discrimination based on race and sexual orientation, as well as discrimination of women on the labour market and in the public sphere, in reproduction rights, and violence against women and domestic violence are issues, which pose a great threat (Burek 2013).

According to reports, the minority group suffering most from discrimination are the Roma people. Their situation is additionally worsened by a difficult social and economic position (Report IV on the situation of national and ethnic minorities and regional languages in the Republic of Poland 2013). Poland undertakes a range of actions to prevent and combat discrimination. Here we should mention *Program for the Roma community in Poland*[4]. Despite the fact that areas of discrimination have been identified, the scope of the problem is difficult to estimate. Discrimination acts often remain unreported and discriminated individuals often fail to identify them.

In Poland there are programs and monitoring of discrimination (for instance *National Action Plan for Equal Treatment*[5]), aiming at combating discrimination based on sex, race, ethnicity, nationality, religion, beliefs, disability, age, and sexual orientation.

4 http://mniejszosci.narodowe.mac.gov.pl/mne/romowie/program-na-rzecz-spole/program-na-rzecz-spole.

5 http://bip.kprm.gov.pl/kpr/bip-rady-ministrow/298,Witamy-na-stronie-Biuletynu-Informacji-Publicznej-Rady-Ministrow.html.

1.2.3 Acceptance of minorities in public life

In view of the results of surveys conducted on representative national-level samples, Poles are characterized by a positive approach towards minority groups. Relatively high level of tolerance towards the presence of a minority in public life is demonstrated in the Eurobarometer study *(Special Eurobarometer 393/2012)* of discrimination. Figure 1.3 shows an average level of acceptance (in Poland and in the European Union) of presence of various minority groups on the highest political posts in Poland filled by elections. Poland is characterized by significantly higher average than the rest of the EU in terms of accepting persons of different religious beliefs, persons with disabilities, or persons from the youngest or oldest age group. A lower level of acceptance is granted to persons of different sexual orientation.

Fig./Tab. 1.3: Acceptance of minorities in public life

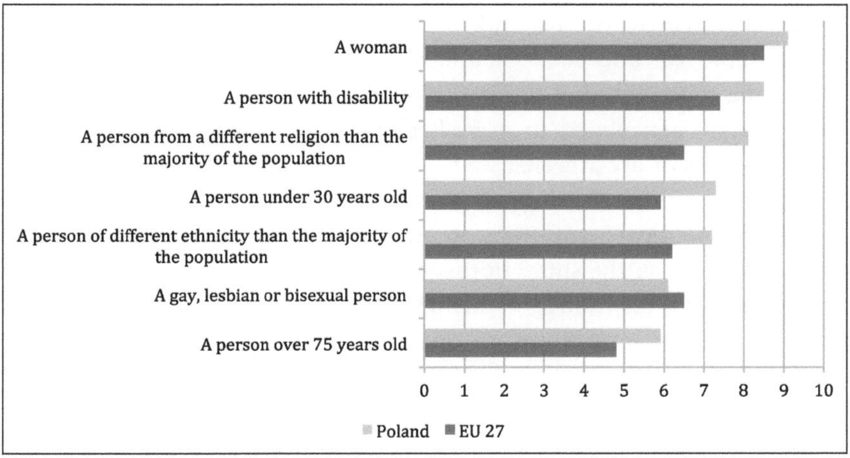

Source: Special Eurobarometer 393/2012

The results of survey research demonstrate that the definition of being Polish is primarily based on cultural and identity features. In accordance with CBOS (Public Opinion Research Centre) (Herrmann 2012), respondents believe that the national community is composed of people who feel Polish (68% of the respondents), speak Polish (52%), and are citizens of Poland (49%). Cultural aspect is also important: 43% stress the importance of having some knowledge of Polish history and culture, whereas preserving Polish traditions and customs is vital for 39% of the respondents. The least important is in the respondents' opinion being Roman Catholic.

Nevertheless, as other studies indicate[6], even 40% personally know someone who was badly treated in Poland because of their ethnic or national origin, or race. Every third Pole admits that they know someone suffering from discrimination based on a disability or religion (Szulecka 2013).

Even though formal equality of political rights gives the society little cause for concern, according to DAP experts the representation of senior citizens is much better than of the youngest grown-ups. Men are better represented than women. Well-educated persons are able to obtain more from the authorities than poorly educated persons. There are no big differences between the way in which interests of rural and urban areas dwellers are represented. An insignificant difference is observed in how much access employees and employers have to the authorities. A vital feature facilitating representation of interests is religion. The interests of Roman Catholics are articulated to a greater extent than those who belong to other religions or are atheists.

Experts also pointed out the groups whose interests are overrepresented by national political institutions; in other words, the groups that have too much influence on the state. In this context the Roman Catholic Church was most often mentioned as an institution that has, in some experts' opinions, diverse possibilities of open or hidden impact on national institutions. The other overrepresented groups are trade unions, employers' organizations, and narrow professional groups.

---

6 A study entitled *Equal Treatment-Standard of Good Governance* by the Jagiellonian University, commissioned by Government Representative for Equal Treatment. The study was conducted in 2011 on a random sample of 1715 adults resident in Poland.

Fig./Tab. 1.4: Representation of interests of various social groups

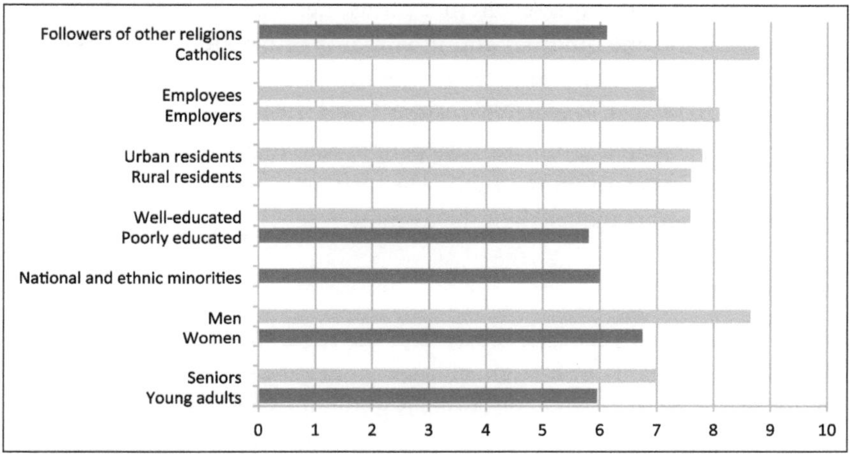

Source: DAP expert survey. Average on a scale from 0 to 10

The level of political representation of various citizen groups can also be analyzed by a comparison of the electoral turnout in selected social and demographic groups with the general turnout of all citizens entitled to vote.

If the turnout in a given group is higher than the average, we say that this specific group is overrepresented in the elections. The data on the basis of which the analyses were prepared come from Polish National Election Study (PGSW) from 2005, 2007 and 2011. The analyses considered the levels of representation of citizen groups divided by social and demographic features.

Persons with a low social and economic status, i.e. badly educated, poorly paid and the unemployed are the most underrepresented. In each of these groups (treated separately) the estimated turnout in the parliamentary elections in 2011 is 11 percentage points lower than the general turnout. Other underrepresented groups include: rural residents, persons who do not practice religion (in both cases the turnout was 7 percentage points lower than the general turnout in 2011) and young people (the turnout was 6 percentage points lower in 2011).

On the other hand, the overrepresented groups in elections include: persons of high social and economic status, i.e. well-educated, with high income (fifth income quintile) and inhabitants of big cities (over 500,000 inhabitants). The difference between the turnout in those groups and the average in 2011 was respectively 13, 12 and 12 percentage points. Another overrepresented group are also people who regularly attend religious service (once a week or more often). The turnout in this group in 2011 was 8 percentage points higher than the average.

1.3 Summary

In case of the situation of non-citizens of the Republic of Poland, failure to ensure political rights of foreigners deserves negative assessment. The possibility of voting in regional elections is granted to citizens of EU member states only and citizens of non-EU states have no voting rights at all.

The system for protection and integration of refugees is assessed positively. Polish legislation implemented international standards in the field of refugee protection. Assessment of the open accommodation centres and regional Departments for Foreigners is improving.

Some problems occur in the process of refugee integration; the most essential one is finding employment. Applicants are too often placed into closed detention centres, which tend to have excessively restrictive regime.

The procedure of acquisition of citizenship by resident foreign nationals changed for the better in 2012, when the bill on Polish citizenship entered into force. In accordance with the existing mechanisms such individuals may acquire citizenship in the course of the administrative procedure.

As regards the rights of citizens belonging to minority groups, the existing legal mechanisms seem to secure their political rights. The scope of discrimination is difficult to assess. According to existing studies the group, Roma people are particularly vulnerable to discrimination.

In representative surveys Poles declare high level of tolerance for minority groups against other EU member states. Poles are in favour of inclusive definition of Polish identity, which means that in order to be recognized as a Pole it is enough to feel Polish and speak the language. Attributes such as being born on the territory of Poland or having Polish parents are of less importance. On the other hand, a significant percentage of Poles declares they know someone who is badly treated or discriminated on the basis of ethnic or racial origin, disability or religion.

Analyses show that interests of some citizen groups are better represented than others. Such groups include: senior citizens, men, well-educated persons, and Roman Catholics. The level of political representation is not the same for all citizens. Persons of high social and economic status (better educated, better paid, and big city dwellers) are better represented.

Bibliography

Analiza zmian dotyczących zasad nabywania obywatelstwa polskiego [An analysis of changes related to regulations for acquisition of Polish citizenship]. Available online on: http://www.emn.gov.pl/esm/aktualnosci/10185,dok.html (accessed on 01.20.2014).

A. Bergiel, K. Kubin, *Bezpłatne poradnictwo prawne dla migrantów przymusowych – opis i ocena działalności organizacji pozarządowych* [Free legal advice for forced migrants – a description and assessment of functionality of NGOs]. Institute of Public Affairs, Warsaw 2009.

M. Bieniecki, I. Jóźwiak, M. Pawlak, *Migranci z Ukrainy na polskim rynku pracy i na rynkach pracy wybranych państw Unii Europejskiej. Analiza materiałów źródłowych* [Immigrants from Ukraine on the Polish labour market and on labour markets of selected EU states. An analysis of source materials], in: *Strategie przetrwania. Intergracja cudzoziemców na polskim rynku pracy* [Survival Strategies. Intergration of foreigners on the Polish labor market], edited by J. Frelak, Institute of Public Affairs, Warsaw 2010, p. 9–44.

Convention and Protocol Relating to the Status of Refugees. Available online on: http://www.unhcr.org/3b66c2aa10.html (accessed on 04.25.2014).

Council of Europe – ETS no. 144 – *Convention on the Participation of Foreigners in Public Life at Local Level* [online]. Available online on: http://conventions.coe.int/Treaty/en/Treaties/Html/144.htm (accessed on 04.25.2014).

J. Frelak, A. Korolec, *Funkcjonowanie Wydziału Spraw Cudzoziemców Mazowieckiego Urzędu Wojewódzkiego w oczach imigrantów* [Functionality of the Departmentsfor Foreigners in the Mazowieckie District

Office in the eyes of immigrants], in: *Przyjazny Urząd. Ewaluacja Funkcjonowania Wydziału Spraw Cudzoziemców Mazowieckiego Urzędu Wojewódzkiego* [Customer-friendly Office. Evaluation of functionality of the Departments for Foreigners in the Mazowieckie District Office], edited by W. Klaus, Association for Legal Intervention, Warsaw 2009, p. 47–72.

A. Gutkowska, *Ewaluacja poradnictwa prawnego dla uchodźców – analiza prawna i praktyczna* [Evaluation of legal advice for refugees -a legal and practical analysis], Institute of Public Affairs, Warsaw 2009.

T. Huddleston, J. Niessen, *Migration Integration Policy Index III, Poland*, British Council and Migration Policy Group 2011.

Ustawa z dnia 13 czerwca 2003 r. o udzielaniu cudzoziemcom ochrony na terytorium Rzeczypospolitej Polskiej [The bill of June 13th 2003 on providing protection for aliens on the territory of the Republic of Poland], Dziennik Ustaw 2003 No. 128 item 1176.

P. Kaźmierczak, J. Seges-Frelak, *Parytycypacja publiczna i prawa polityczne obywateli państw trzecich na szczeblu krajowym i lokalnym* [Public participation and political rights of citizens of third countries on the national and local level], in: *W poszukiwaniu nowych wzroców integracji cudzoziemców. Wybór Tekstów Polskiego Forum Integracyjnego* [In search for new patterns of alien integration. Selected Articles in Polish Integration Forum]. Institute of Public Affairs, edited by J. Seges-Frelak, K. Grot, Warsaw 2013, p. 13–38.

Migracja to nie zbrodnia. Raport z monitoringu strzeżonych ośrodków dla cudzoziemców [Migration Is Not a Crime. A Report on monitoring of guarded centres for foreigners], Association for Legal Intervention, Helsinki Foundation of Human Rights, Warsaw 2012.

Participatory Assessment 2010 Report, *Being a refugee. How refugees and asylum-seekers experience life in Central Europe*, United Nations High Commissioner for Refugees, Budapest 2011.

M. Pawlak, *Imitacja w tworzeniu polskiej polityki integracji cudzoziemców* [Fake creation of Polish policy of integrating foreigners], "Migr. Study-Polish Overview." 2013, 97–121.

Polish Migration Policy – current state and postulated actions. A ECRI Report on Poland. The fourth monitoring cycle, European Commision against Racism and Intolerance 2010.

T. Sieniow, *Wnioski z monitoringu wraz z rekomendacjami*, in: *Stosowanie Detencji Wobec Cudzoziemców. Raport z monitoringu i rekomendacje*, edited by T. Sieniow, the Rule of Law Institute, Lublin 2013.

G. Szymańska-Matusiewicz, *Funkcjonowanie Wydziału Spraw Cudzoziemców Mazowieckiego Urzędu Wojewódzkiego w oczach cudzoziemców*, in: *Przyjaźniejszy urząd? Ewaluacja funkcjonowania wydziału spraw cudzoziemców mazowieckiego urzędu wojewódzkiego w 2012 roku*, edited by N. Korek, W. Klaus, Association for Legal Intervention, Warsaw 2012, p. 37–68.

2. The rule of law

In our definition of the rule of law, three factors are of primary importance, namely: the quality of legislation, institutional infrastructure (organization and effectiveness of courts and the public prosecutor's office) as well as prestige of law (compliance with the applicable legal provisions and the level of tolerance for actions resulting in breaking the law).

2.1 International context: general assessment of the rule of law in Poland

An overview of the rule of law should start with placing this problem in the international context in order to provide it with a reference point for the data obtained in Poland.

According to a study by the World Bank known as *World Governance Indicators,* measuring the quality of enforcement of the contracts, property rights, performance of the police forces and the judiciary, as well as crime and violence levels[7], Poland scored 0.74 points (on a scale from –2.5 to 2.5). This assessment is comparable to other countries similar in their social, economic and political development.

When we look at the dynamics of the assessment of the rule of law in Poland, it will turn out that until 1998 this indicator was increasing and then until 2006 it was decreasing only to go up again, and in 2012 reached the similar level to the previous peak of 1998.

7 A detailed overview of the methodology and the results is available on http://info.worldbank.org/governance/wgi/index.aspx#doc (accessed on 01.16.2014).

Fig./Tab. 2.1: The rule of law indicator

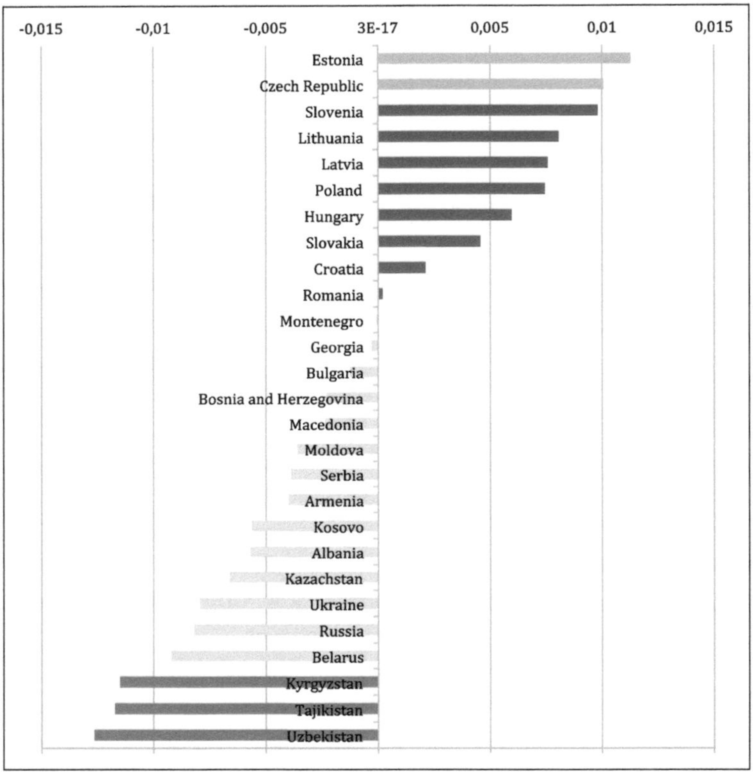

Source: World Bank

2.2 The law-making process

The Polish legislative process is described in the Articles 118 up to 123 of the Constitution as well as in the Sejm regulations, and a number of other legal acts of various levels. A poignant description of[8] its aberrations might be found in the government report *Poland 2030* whose authors state that

8 *Biała Księga – 35 rekomendacji, do których realizacji nowy rząd powinien przystąpić w pierwszym roku działalności* [White Book – 35 recommendations whose implementation the new government should undertake during the first year of its functioning], PKPP (Polish Confederation) Lewiatan, 2011, p. 7.

"in the Polish law-making process (...) the formal approach is dominant. (...) [T]he usually fast pace of works and low quality of lawmaking process organization result in creating law of high quantity and low quality."[9]

A spectacular illustration of this process is a simple comparison of the algorithm for proceeding legislation recommended by OECD to the Polish practice.

Fig./Tab. 2.2: A comparison of the process of preparing regulation projects in accordance with the OECD guidelines (the left side) to the Polish practice (the right side)

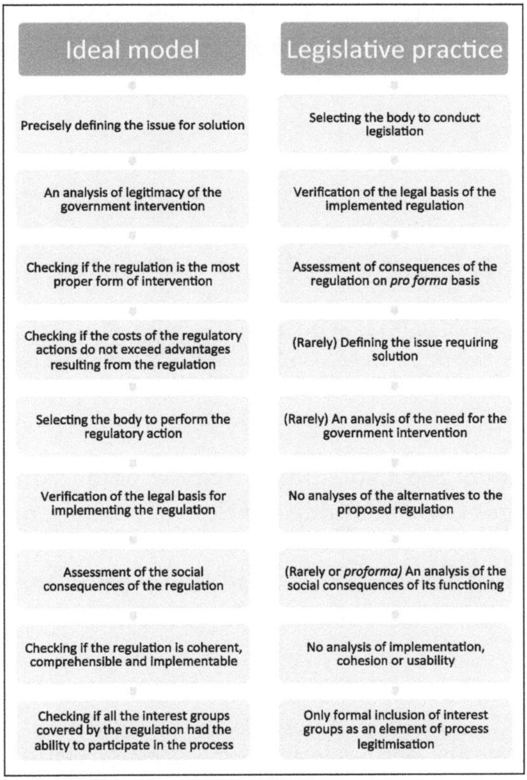

Source: Polska 2030, p. 310–311

---

9 *Polska 2030. Wyzwania rozwojowe* [Poland 2030. Development challenges], Warsaw: Chancellary of thePrime Minister, 2009, p. 311.

2.2.1 The quality of law

Since mid-1990s there has been an inflation of the law regulations (Fig./Tab. 2.3). The amount of adopted law to a great extent results from the necessity of adjusting it to the EU norms (a record value for this indicator was noted in the year of Poland's accession to the EU when the Union law had to be implemented in the Polish regulations). Nevertheless, new bills and amendments introduced within harmonization of the Polish law with the Union law often contradict existing law or they duplicate it[10].

Fig./Tab. 2.3: Annual volume of the Dziennik Ustaw11 (in pages) of 1989–2011

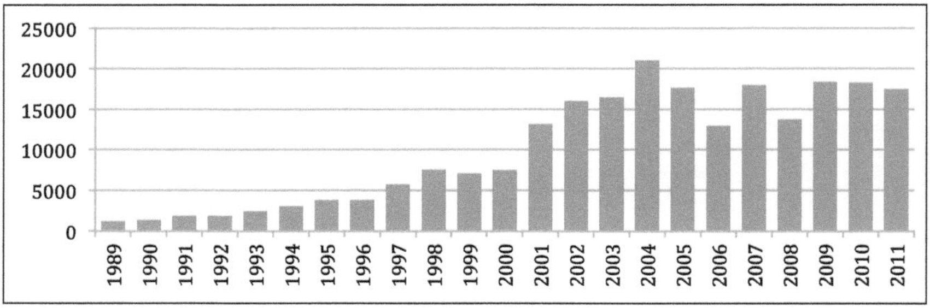

Source: Own statement on the basis of the data obtained from www.dziennikustaw.gov.pl (printing of the Dziennik Ustaw stopped in 2012 and, as a consequence, page numbering was abolished)

Taking into account the amount of ceaselessly produced law, it is hardly a surprise that this law is sometimes unclear or contrary to the other legal acts.

A necessity to eliminate mistakes leads to frequent amendments which constitute the majority of laws adopted by the Sejm.

10 For instance the bill of January 20th 2011 on asset liability of publicly appointed office-holders for gross violation of the law (*Ustawa z dnia 2011 stycznia 2011 r. o odpowiedzialności majątkowej funkcjonariuszy publicznych za rażące naruszenie prawa*), Dziennik Ustaw 2011 No. 34, item 173.

11 Official journal containing all legislation of the Republic of Poland. Promulgation of bills in *Dziennik Ustaw* is necessary for them to come into force.

Fig./Tab. 2.4: Assessment of law made by the Sejm

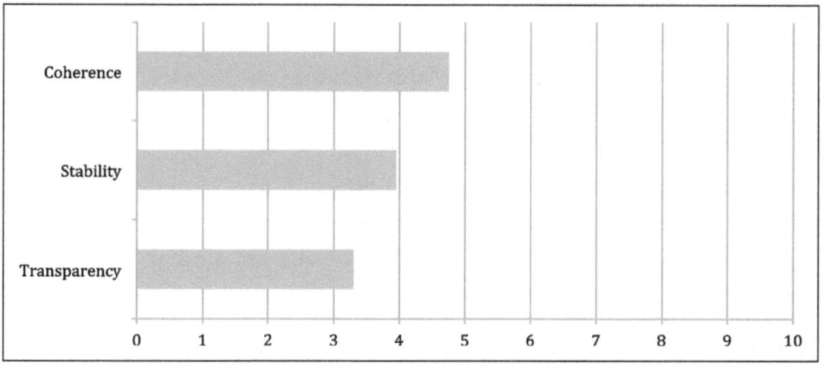

Source: DAP expert survey. Average on a scale from 0 to10

The critical assessment of the legislative process and the quality of bills is confirmed in opinions of DAP experts. In relation to all the three aspects we enquired about (coherence, stability, clarity) Polish bills were low-rated, that is below 5 points on a scale of 0-10.

2.3 Independence of the judicial system

Another matter raised in the expert survey were guarantees of independence of the judicial system. According to specialists, in Poland there are strong legal and actual guarantees of independence of the judicial system

Fig./Tab. 2.5: The assessment of independence of the judicial system

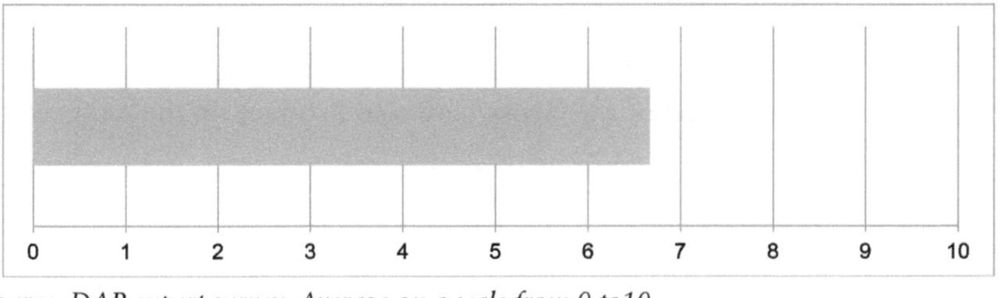

Source: DAP expert survey. Average on a scale from 0 to10

According to DAP experts, the situations in which a politician or an official is trying to informally influence the court proceedings are rare. Among examples of interventions the experts pointed at the connections between elites on the local level, where judiciary could be reached informally. Both the connections between lawyers and other circles and business interests of the legal community may play a role in deciding court cases.

2.4 Performance of the judiciary

The assessment of the effectiveness of the judiciary (courts of law and the public prosecutor's office) was conducted with the help of all the three methods applied in this study. The results are similar but not fully consistent.

2.4.1 Poland v. Europe: efficiency of the judiciary

A study called *Evaluation of European Judicial Systems* is conducted on a regular basis by the European Commission for the Efficiency of Justice (CEPEJ), at the Council of Europe. The latest report was issued in 2012 on the basis of the data from 2010. In this study Poland did well with respect to the economic foundations of the judiciary.

The state assigns a substantial part of GDP and the courts have numerous judges at their disposal. The problem is equality of legal access as the resources for providing necessary legal aid to individuals unable to afford an attorney are very limited. There is no comprehensive system of legal aid for those in need.

The economic foundations of functioning of the judiciary

If we compare countries of Europe in terms of public expenditure on the courts, the public prosecutor's office, and legal aid Poland can be found among the leaders. Only the countries of the former Yugoslavia and Bulgaria assign a greater part of the Gross National Product on the judiciary[12].

12 *Evaluation of European Judicial Systems*, 2012 [online]. Available online on: The European Commission for the Efficiency of Justice. http://www.coe.int/t/dghl/cooperation/cepej/evaluation/ (accessed on 11.22.2013), p. 55.

Fig./Tab. 2.6: Total expenditure on the judiciary (courts, the public prosecutor's office, legal aid) as % of GDP per capita in various European countries

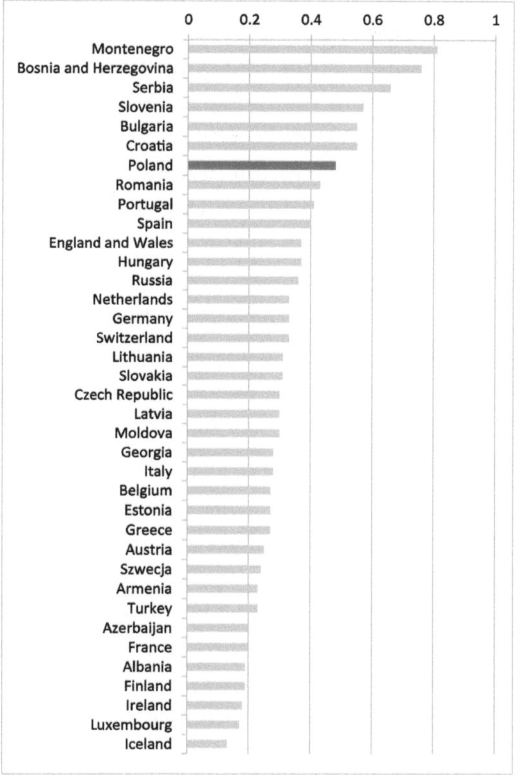

Source: CEPEJ

Another measure of the economic position might be staffing of the judiciary. According to the experts of CEPEJ, "[G]enerally speaking, in the legal systems of Central and Eastern Europe the proportion of the number of judges to the population is higher than in Western Europe."[13] The European average for this indicator is 21.3 of professional judges per 100,000 people. In Poland it is 27.8. These differences partially result from the lower number of jurors in the eastern than in the western part of the continent.

13 Ibid, p. 146.

Effectivity of the judiciary: average time of enforcement of contract claims

Effectivity of the judiciary in economic matters is measured in a study known as *Doing Business* conducted by the World Bank. The indicator[14] used in DAP demonstrates the time of enforcement of claims arising from contracts by legal means from the moment of submitting the suit by the seller until the time of recovery of the debt.

Poland occupies a low 55th position in the world when it comes to the time needed for recovery of the debt, which is almost 2 years.

Court experts

From an overview published by the Helsinski Foundation for Human Rights, the Stefan Batory Foundation, and the Polish Business Council[15] we can learn that functioning of court experts constitutes one of the most severe shortcomings of the judiciary in Poland. The authors of the overview point to the following significant problems and areas for correction:

- functioning of court-appointed experts and specialist institutions is currently underregulated;
- the system of selecting individuals or institutions requested to prepare opinions for preliminary and court proceedings fails to guarantee high professional standard of the candidates;
- current recording system does not produce the full picture of the scientific and specialist potential of the experts available for the judiciary bodies;
- remuneration system does not serve as an incentive for the specialists of highest professional standards to work as court experts;

14 Used by GUS (the Central Statistical Office) under Monitoring of Development System, see: http://strateg.stat.gov.pl/Home/Strateg.

15 B. Grabowska, A. Pietryka, M. Wolny, and A. Bodnar (scientific cooperation), *Eksperci sądowi w Polsce* [Court experts in Poland], the Helsinki Foundation for Human Rights, the Stefan Batory Foundation and the Polish Business Council, 2014, p. 2.

- in spite of the fact that the opinions are often of low quality in terms of professional standards, courts value them highly, and treat them as more reliable evidence than others;
- it is necessary to change bad practices of the judiciary bodies when it comes to appointing experts.

2.4.2 Expert assessment of functioning of the judiciary

Judges are rated highest in the assessment of the judiciary. Courts as institutions are assessed less favorably.

Fig./Tab. 2.7: Assessment of the judiciary

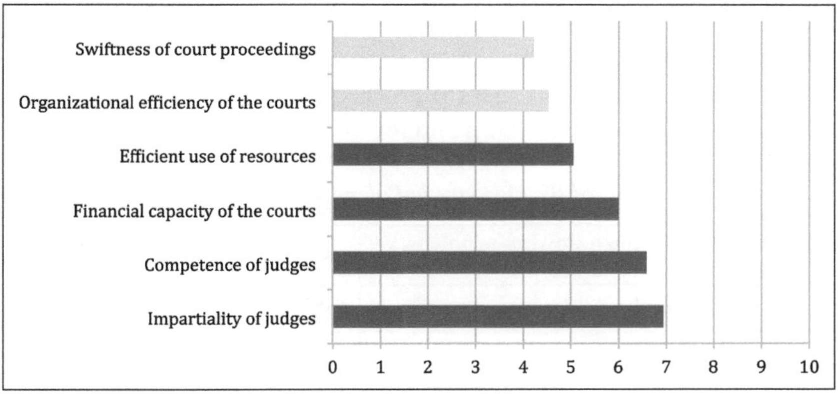

Source: DAP expert survey. Average on a scale from 0 to10

2.4.3 Social assessment of the functioning of the judiciary[16]

Social assessment of the functioning of the judiciary is rather negative (Boguszewski 2013).

16 Based on CBOS survey from Nov-Dec. 2012, N=1135 adult representatives resident in Poland.

Fig./Tab. 2.8: Social assessment of the functioning of the judiciary

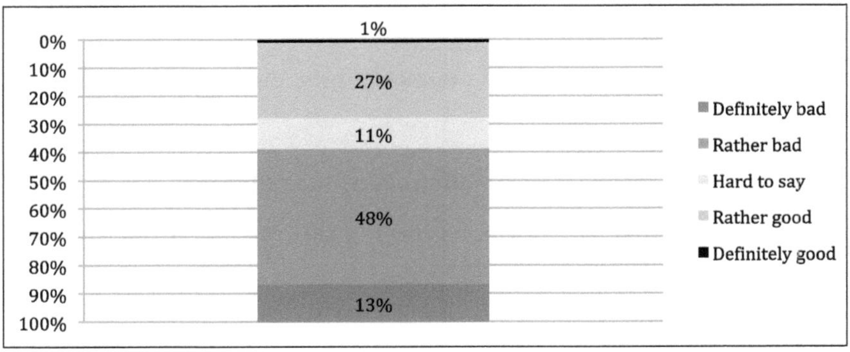

Source: CBOS

The most commonly mentioned problems in functioning of the judiciary include unreasonable length of the court proceedings (mentioned by 84% of the respondents), the fact that the proceedings are often delayed (72%), too high costs of the proceedings and too complex procedures.

Fig./Tab. 2.9: Problems of the judiciary in Poland according to the public opinion

Do you think that the following problems concern the judiciary in Poland	Yes	No	Hard to say
unreasonable length of the court proceedings	84%	4%	12%
delays of the proceedings	72%	10%	18%
excessive costs related to the court proceedings	72%	9%	19%
excessively complex procedures of the court proceedings	71%	9%	20%
ailing system of information flow between courts	62%	10%	28%
too lenient punishment for crimes	60%	19%	21%
unsatisfactory organization of court work	59%	14%	27%
judgement on the basis of insufficient evidence	58%	16%	26%
corruption of judges	54%	17%	29%

too low level of court IT systems	48%	22%	30%
improper behaviour of court officials to citizens	48%	28%	24%
judges breaching legislation when applying procedures	42%	21%	37%
judge incompetence	41%	31%	28%
nepotism when selecting jurors	34%	23%	43%
abuse of pre-trial detention	34%	36%	30%
too rare use of pre-trial detention	31%	38%	31%
insufficient number of judges	28%	42%	30%
understaffing in the court administration	23%	43%	34%
too severe punishments for crimes	14%	65%	21%
too low salaries of judges	7%	64%	29%

Source: CBOS

Courts and the Public Prosecutor's Office

Both the courts and the public prosecutor's office are assessed rather negatively[17]. The assessment of performance of the courts gradually improved from 2005, and in 2011 there was a sudden fall of satisfaction with the courts. In 2013, 50% of Poles negatively assessed the courts, whereas a third of respondents believed the courts were functioning well. The situation is quite similar in the case of the public prosecutor's office.

Confidence in the judiciary

Confidence in the judiciary in Poland (average 3.66[18]) is one of the lowest in Europe. It is shown in the high percentage of Poles declaring more confidence in the ruling of the European Court of Human Rights in Strasbourg (72%) than the ruling of the national courts (14%).

17 On the basis of monthly reports of CBOS.

18 Average value of the response on a scale of 11 points, where 0 means lack of confidence and 10 complete confidence.

Fig./Tab. 2.10: Confidence in the judiciary of citizens of European countries

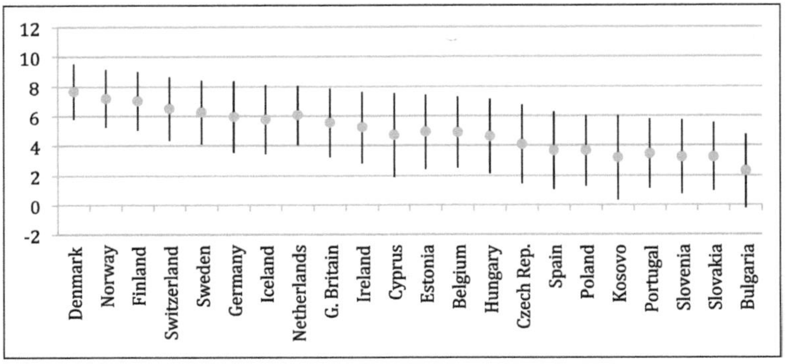

Source: European Social Survey

2.4.4 Access to law

The amount of public resources for legal aid is a measure of the intensity of the actions of the authorities to ensure access to the judiciary for all members of society. Yet the state provides access to free legal aid only on the court level. It is accessible for low-income individuals in the form of a public defence solicitor. However, there are no solutions to guarantee citizens access to free legal aid during the pre- trial phase[19].

The factor that exacerbates the weakness of the legal system is lack of clarity in legal regulations and absence of infrastructure for citizens to access legal information. According to a study by INPRIS (Law and Society Institute), "the existing legal regulations regarding announcement of normative acts, the rules regulating access to public information, as well as practice of public institutions fail to provide enough tools enabling citizen access to complete, up to date and clear knowledge on the applicable law."[20]

19 An overview of this issue can be found in: J. Winczorek, *Przegląd literatury na temat dostępności i korzystania z pomocy prawnej* [An overview of literature on availability and usage of legal aid]. Warsaw: Instytut Prawa i Społeczeństwa 2012.

20 *Powszechny dostęp do aktów prawnych i orzeczeń sądowych* [Universal access to legal acts and judicial decisions], Instytut Prawa i Społeczeństwa, December 2010 [online]. Available online on http://www.inpris.pl/fileadmin/user_upload/documents/pomoc_prawna/Powszechny_dostep_do_aktow_prawnych_i_orzeczen_sadowych.pdf (accessed on 20.03.2014).

International comparisons

European countries differ greatly in terms of the range of legal aid for their citizens. Countries of Northern and Western Europe as well as Bosnia and Herzegovina are doing a great deal of work in this area. Most of the countries of Central and Eastern Europe are on the opposite pole. Poland belongs to the countries that assign a small portion of GDP to ensuring access to law to those individuals who cannot afford an attorney or a solicitor[21].

Fig./Tab. 2.11: Expenditure on legal aid per citizen in various European countries in (% GDP per capita)

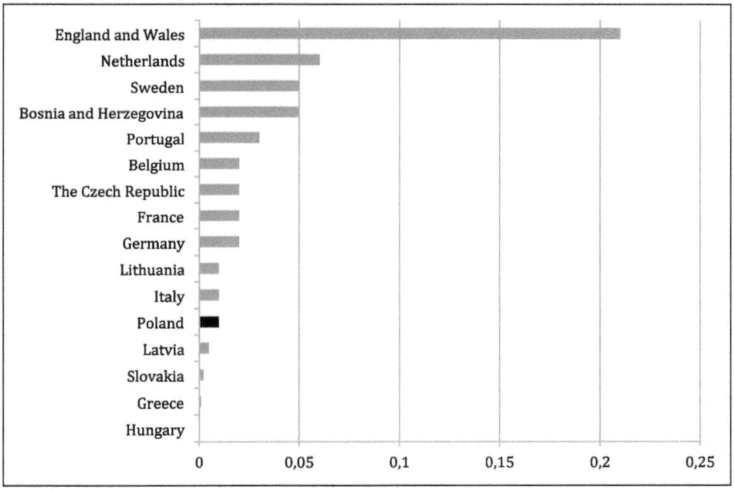

Source: CEPEJ

Expert opinions

According to experts, as a rule the courts treat citizens equally, which does not mean that all citizens have equal access to the law. The factors limiting actual access are complex procedures difficult for citizens with low level of education and limited cognitive and cultural competences, as well as low legal culture in the society, and a lack of awareness of the rules governing the judiciary.

21 *Evaluation of European Judicial Systems*, p. 46.

Fig./Tab. 2.12: Assessment of equality before the law

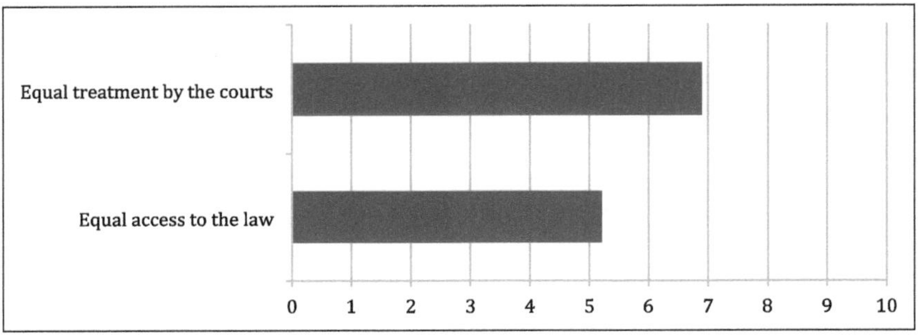

Source: DAP expert survey. Average of a scale from 0 to10

2.5 Legal culture in the society

Public opinion polls show societal attitude to respecting the law. They provide us with information on the prestige of law.

2.5.1 Respect for the law[22]

Poles' approach to respecting the law is assessed negatively. According to 51% of respondents, the majority of ordinary people often do not respect the law, whereas according to 44%, the majority usually obey the law. Even 57% of respondents believe that the law in Poland is enforced less strictly than several years back.

2.5.2 Attitude towards public goods and morality[23]

Poles' attitude towards public goods is not assessed very positively.

22 CBOS survey from Nov-Dec 2012, N=1135 on a sample representatives for adult residents of Poland.

23 CBOS survey from Oct. 2012, N=1007, on a sample representative for adult residents of Poland.

Fig./Tab. 2.13: Perceived attitude towards the law and public goods

Do you think people in Poland generally:	Yes	No	Hard to say
respect publicly owned property	29%	64%	7%
are willing to compromise–can reduce their needs in order to consider others' interests	32%	59%	9%
pay taxes honestly	35%	56%	9%
can cooperate and do things collectively	46%	46%	8%

Source: CBOS – Hipsz 2012

Respondents were also asked to express their attitude to a range of behaviours encountered in social and private life, which might be regarded as wrong or raise objections[24]. The study demonstrated particular social acceptance of fiscal crimes and offences.

Fig./Tab. 2.14: Acceptance of unlawful or unacceptable behaviour

	Doesn't bother me at all	Rather doesn't bother me	Rather bothers me	Bothers me a lot	Average
Someone dumps their household rubbish in the forest	2%	2%	8%	88%	5.76 (0.84)
Someone disposes of untreated sewage water in the nearest river or lake	2%	2%	12%	84%	5.68 (0.92)
Someone drives when being tipsy, intoxicated	2%	3%	11%	84%	5.67 (0.96)
Someone doesn't clean after their dog	3%	6%	22%	67%	5.32 (1.23)
Someone throws rubbish in random places	3%	10%	28%	59%	5.14 (1.30)

24 The variable measured on a scale from 1 to 6 where 1 means that given behaviour does not bother them at all and does not interest them, whereas 6 means it bothers them a lot and raises their objections. The option "Hard to say" was excluded from the analysis.

	Doesn't bother me at all	Rather doesn't bother me	Rather bothers me	Bothers me a lot	Average
A local councillor fails to show up for their office hours	8%	8%	27%	53%	4.91 (1.57)
An official takes care of private matters during their working hours	6%	11%	30%	51%	4.90 (1.51)
Someone jumps the queue for a visit to a public specialist doctor	8%	11%	27%	52%	4.83 (1.60)
Someone receives the unemployment benefit despite being employed	11%	11%	24%	52%	4.71 (1.74)
A driver breaks speed limits	7%	15%	32%	46%	4.69 (1.56)
Someone pays less tax than they should	9%	14%	30%	44%	4.60 (1.66)
Someone manages to avoid paying electricity bills	14%	11%	25%	48%	4.57 (1.82)
Someone disturbs their neighbours between 10pm and 6am	9%	16%	31%	43%	4.56 (1.66)
Someone crosses the road on the red light	13%	18%	20%	48%	4.43 (1.85)
Someone drinks alcohol in a public place	11%	18%	28%	42%	4.42 (1.75)
Someone submits false medical certificate to avoid work	13%	16%	27%	42%	4.36 (1.82)
Someone imports goods without paying customs	15%	20%	26%	45%	4.11 (1.87)
Someone avoids paying administrative fees on the flat	18%	18%	27%	33%	4.02 (1.89)
Someone smokes at the bus stop	26%	18%	22%	34%	3.74 (2.04)
Someone fails to pay their bus, tram or train fare	23%	21%	26%	28%	3.68 (1.95)

Someone lets the tap drop in their household	24%	24%	24%	26%	3.57 (1.94)
Someone buys cheaper cigarettes or alcohol with no excise duty	32%	20%	21%	24%	3.29 (2.01)
Someone keeps overdue library books	24%	29%	26%	18%	3.27 (1.82)
Someone fails to pay the audiovisual license fee	37%	22%	19%	19%	2.97 (1.96)
Someone works illegally	37%	28%	18%	14%	2.78 (1.83)
Someone registers their child at their friends' to get a place in the nearest school	38%	25%	17%	13%	2.73 (1.83)

Source: CBOS

2.6 Civil liberties

According to specialists, Poland is a free country if we consider the freedom of establishing and joining associations as well as the right of assembly. Both legal protection and practice were highly assessed.

Fig./Tab. 2.15: Assessment of civil liberties protection

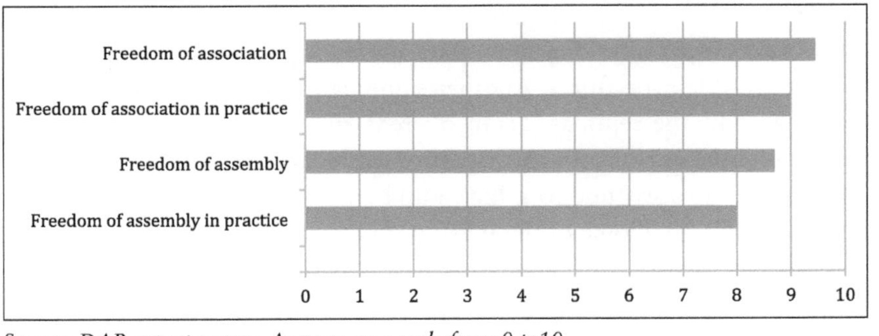

Source: DAP expert survey. Average on a scale from 0 to10

Ombudsman's activity

The institution safeguarding freedom, human and civil rights in Poland is the Ombudsman. The office is respected by citizens who are aware of the institution's functioning (even though members of society are not very familiar with it). According to studies by CBOS, 39% of adult Poles positively assess the Ombudsman, 16% see it negatively, and 45% have no opinion on the functioning of this institution[25].

2.7 Summary

Assessment of Polish democracy with regards to the quality of the rule of law is ambivalent. It seems that formal systemic solutions might be assessed better than the practice of functioning of the institutions. Generally speaking, the rule of law operates in Poland. The law is made as a result of democratic procedures. The fundamental civil rights are respected. Poland presents itself satisfactorily against other countries of similar social and political conditions.

Regarding material foundations of functioning of the judiciary, Poland occupies a high position among European countries. The state assigns substantial part of its GDP to courts and the public prosecutor's office, and employment is high. The economic position of judges is satisfactory.

Assessment of the performance of the courts of law is rather poor. They are badly organized and ineffective. Unreasonable length of court proceedings is a very acute problem, noticed by the vast majority of the society, experts interviewed by DAP and external experts. Enforcing trade agreements takes especially long time, partially owing to complicated and incomprehensible procedures. Another significant problem is the quality of law created by the Sejm, as it is incoherent, incomprehensible, and unstable. One of the reasons for this situation is the fact that this is most often a bottom-up process due to a high number of MPs' amendments, which disrupt the internal logic of the bills.

There are significant inequalities in access to the law. The state does little to facilitate using the judiciary by the poorest members of society. Complicated procedures require significant cultural and intellectual powers unavailable for many members of society.

---

25 http://cbos.pl/SPISKOM.POL/2012/K_128_12.PDF.

Social foundations of the rule of law are weak. Public opinion holds that a high number of members of the society do not respect the law and, at the same time, that many Poles accept unlawful activities.

Bibliography

Biała Księga – 35 rekomendacji, do których realizacji nowy rząd powinien przystąpić w pierwszym roku działalności [White Book – 35 recommendations whose implementation the new government should undertake during the first year of its functioning], PKPP (Polish Confederation) Lewiatan, 2011.

R. Boguszewski, *O przestrzeganiu prawa I funkcjonowaniu wymiaru sprawiedliwości w Polsce* [On respecting the law and functioning of the judiciary in Poland], a report by CBOS [online]. Available online on: http://www.cbos.pl/SPISKOM.POL/2013/K_005_13.PDF (accessed on 03.18.2013).

Doing Business 2013 [online]. Available online on: http://www.doingbusiness.org/methodology/enforcing-contracts (accessed on 11.22.2013).

Evaluation of European Judicial Systems, 2012 [online]. Available online on: http://www.coe.int/t/dghl/cooperation/cepej/evaluation/ (accessed on 11.22.2013).

B. Grabowska, A. Pietryka, M. Wolny and A. Bodnar (scientific cooperation), *Biegli sądowi w Polsce* [Court experts in Poland], Helsinki Foundation for Human Rights, Stefan Batory Foundation, and the Polish Business Council 2014.

N. Hipsz, *O dobrach wspólnych I moralności publicznej* [On common goods and public morality], a report by CBOS 2012 [online]. Available online on: http://www.cbos.pl/SPISKOM.POL/2012/K_155_12.PDF (accessed on 02.20. 2013).

N. Hipsz, *Ocena instytucji publicznych* [Assessment of public insitutions], a report by CBOS 2012 http://cbos.pl/SPISKOM.POL/2012/K_128_12.PDF, (accessed on 4.9.2014).

Mechanizmy przeciwdziałania korupcji w Polsce [Mechanisms to combat corruption in Poland], Institute of Publjc Affairs [online]. Available online on: http://www.isp.org.pl/strona-glowna,mechanizmyprzeciwdzialania-korupcji-w-polsce,rzecznik-praw-obywatelskich,772.html (accessed on 4.9.2010).

Polska 2030. Wyzwania rozwojowe [Poland 2030. Development challenges], Warsaw: Office of Prime Minister, 2009.

Powszechny dostęp do aktów prawnych i orzeczeń sądowych [Universal access to legal acts and judicial decisions], Instytut Prawa i Społeczeństwa, December 2010.

J. Winczorek, *Przegląd literatury na temat dostępności i korzystania z pomocy prawnej* [An overview of literature on availability and usage of legal aid]. Warsaw: Instytut Prawa i Społeczeństwa 2012.

World Governance Indicators [online]. Available online on: http://info.worldbank.org/governance/wgi/index.aspx#doc (accessed on 12.07.2013).

Zielona księga: system stanowienia prawa w Polsce [Green Book: Law-making system in Poland]. Office of the President of the Republic of Poland and Public Debate Forum, Warsaw 2013.

3. The media

The mass media constitute an indispensable element for enforcing the accountability of authorities. Objective and accurate knowledge of activities of institutions and political elites allows members of the society to act in order to correct policies or change the government. It is worth stressing that the media interest us only as a source of information on the public sphere, especially political institutions.

3.1 Freedom of speech

Legal and actual freedom of speech is fundamental for the smooth functioning of democracy. The audit of the situation of the media in Poland should start with a comparison with countries in a similar political and economic situation (EU member states from Central and Eastern Europe).

3.1.1 International context

If we consider the condition of the Polish media within international context, the assessment is positive. According to a report by Freedom House entitled *Freedom of the Press,* the media in Poland are free. Among Central and Eastern European countries belonging to the European Union the media have the same status in Estonia, the Czech Republic, Slovenia, Slovakia, Lithuania, and Latvia. The situation of the media in the remaining four countries (in Hungary, Bulgaria, Croatia, and Romania) is worse as they are partially free[26].

The negative factors include the regulations on libel (Art. 212 of the Penal Code), as well as the regulations on defamation of religion and insulting the head of the state. Experts also point out cases of owner interference in the editorial line of some newspapers. They also note weak economic foundations of the public media, which is related to low level of payment of audiovisual licence fee.

---

26 *Freedom of the Press 2013* [online] available online on: http://www.freedomhouse.org/report-types/freedom-press (accessed on 12.13.2013).

Economic problems concern the whole sector of the media that, owing to decreasing popularity, are forced to limit their functions and downsize.

Fig./Tab. 3.1: Freedom of the media in the countries of Eastern and Central Europe belonging to the European Union (lower values indicate more freedom)

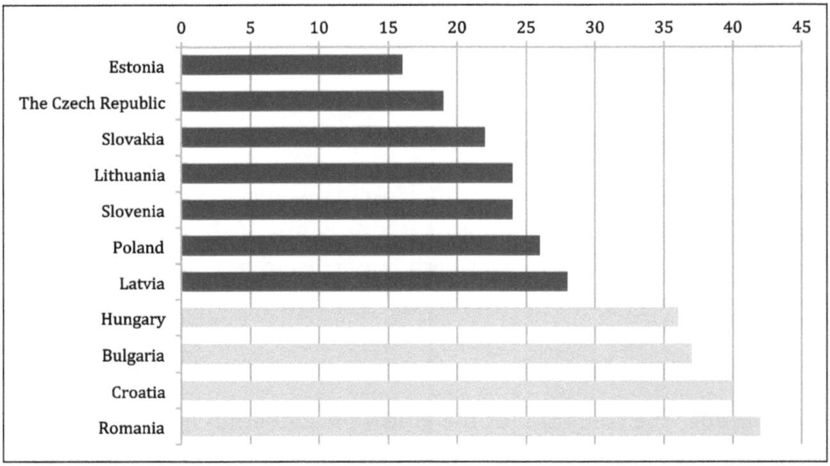

Source: Freedom House – Freedom of the Press

Another international study of freedom of the press is annually conducted by a French organization *Reporters Without Borders*. This is the so-called Freedom of the Press Index[27].

Similarly to the results of the Freedom House Index with regards to freedom of press, the situation in Poland is regarded as satisfactory. Among the countries of the region only Estonia and the Czech Republic noted better results.

3.1.2 Freedom of speech according to DAP experts

Poland is a country where freedom of speech is respected. Legal guarantees of freedom of speech were assessed very highly, whereas the practice is slightly worse, but also quite positive.

27 http://en.rsf.org/spip.php?page=classement&id_rubrique=1054,(accessed on 12.13.2013).

The most commonly mentioned economic restrictions on freedom are the requirements of the free market. The press is especially susceptible to these limitations, which is related to decreasing circulation. The media are dependent on advertisers, which results in self-censorship, especially in the case of investigative journalism. Some experts pointed at legal barriers (Article 212 of the Penal Code) related to libel. The law that allows local authorities to publish press, which destroys the market, is also criticized.

Fig./Tab. 3.2: Assessment of freedom of speech

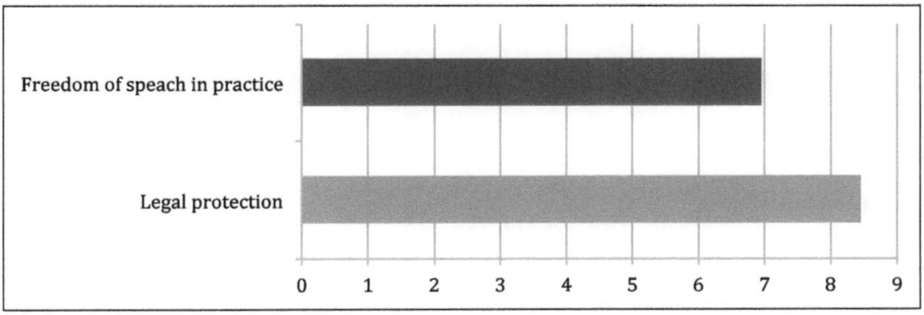

Source: DAP expert survey. Average of a scale from 0 to 10

An important element of the freedom of the media is their independence from political pressure. This situation in case of the private media looks more optimistic than the public. It might be related to the institutional position of TVP (Polish public TV broadcaster) and PR (Polish public radio), which results in politically motivated staff appointments.

Fig./Tab. 3.3: Assessment of political interference in the media

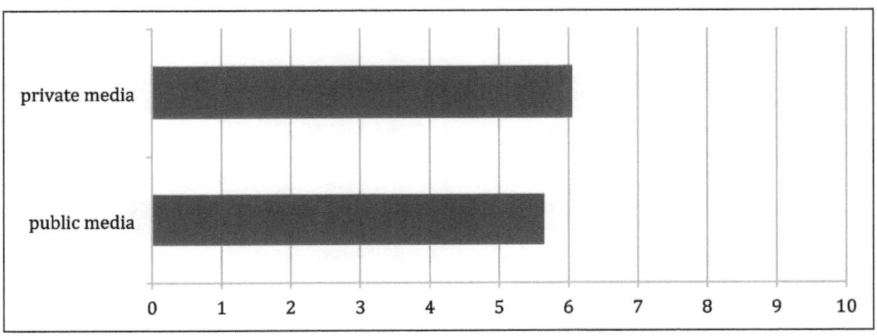

Source: DAP expert survey. Average on a scale from 0 to 10

Another aspect of freedom of the media is the freedom from interference in the content caused by economic factors. These are situations in which the decision to broadcast some material is taken by the owners under pressure of advertisers, or is motivated by other business considerations.

The public media face this pressure to a less extent, whereas in case of the private media the situation looks much worse, even though interference of the owners in the materials is not universal.

Fig./Tab. 3.4: Assessment of freedom from economic pressure

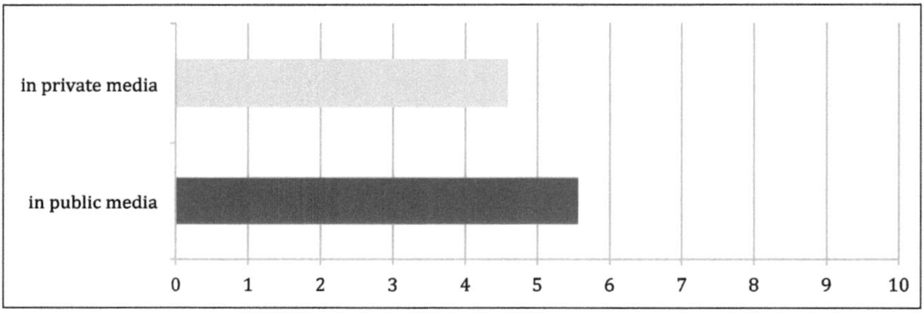

Source: DAP expert survey. Average on a scale from 0 to 10

Fig./Tab. 3.5: Assessment of freedom from interference of the media owners

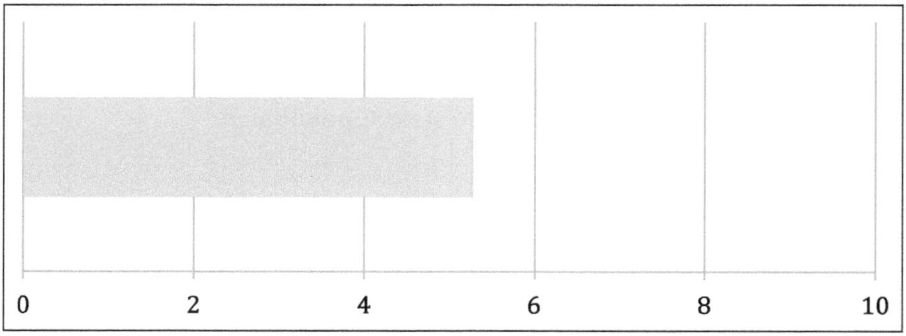

Source: DAP expert survey. Average on a scale from 0 to 10

3.2 The quality of information on the public sphere

Media are important for us as a source of information on the public sphere. Their quality determines whether members of the society are able to take the best possible electoral decision.

3.2.1 International context

A study that helps contextualize the quality of the news in the Polish media is the Sustainable Governance Indicators project (SGI[28]), prepared by the Bertelsmann Foundation. It aims to define areas that require a reform of the institutional system in the member states of OECD. One of the SGI dimensions of the quality of democracy is citizen access to information on the public sphere.

Against the other OECD countries, Poland occupies a relatively high position as it was included in a group of countries which respect freedom of speech, although sometimes limited by the government. The situation in Poland is comparable to that of the Czech Republic.

Fig./Tab. 3.6: Assessment of access to information in various countries (according to Sustainable Governance Index 2011)

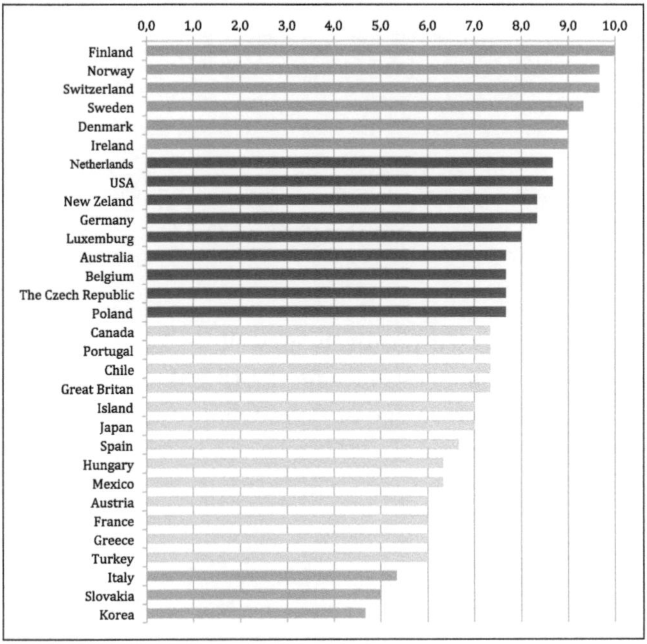

Source: Sustainable Governance Indicators 2011

28 http://www.sgi-network.org/index.php., (accessed on 11.01.2014).

3.2.2 Assessment of radio and television in the surveys conducted on a representative sample of the population[29]

Assessment of the three main public and private television broadcasters by citizens is good. Despite numerous differences between the public television and private stations (TVN and Polsat), a similar percentage (almost 80%) of Poles assess them positively.

The opinion concerning particular stations is subject to slight fluctuations over time. It is interesting that, during the last year, the three stations improved their scores after several years of continuous downward trend.

Fig./Tab. 3.7: Assessment of television channels (pct. of positive opinions)

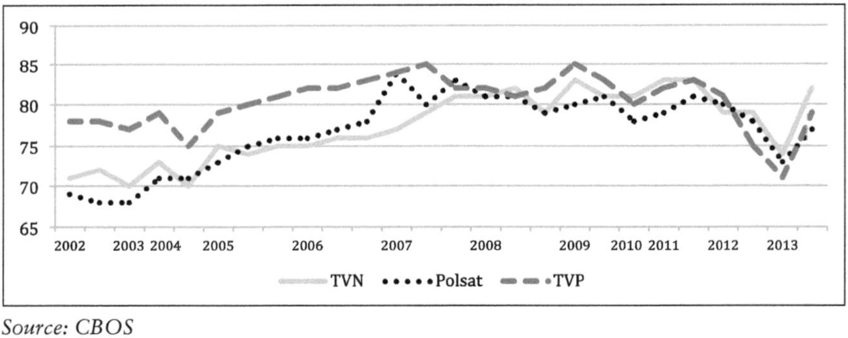

Source: CBOS

Radio stations are assessed positively as well. In 2013 the percentage of positive evaluations of the Polish Radio, RMF FM and Radio ZET was at the rate of 70%. The percentage of Poles who positively assess these stations gradually increased until 2007, whereas in the last few years there has been no discernible trend.

29 On the basis of the results obtained in CBOS surveys on samples representative for the adult population.

Fig./Tab. 3.8: Assessment of the radio stations (pct. of positive opinions)

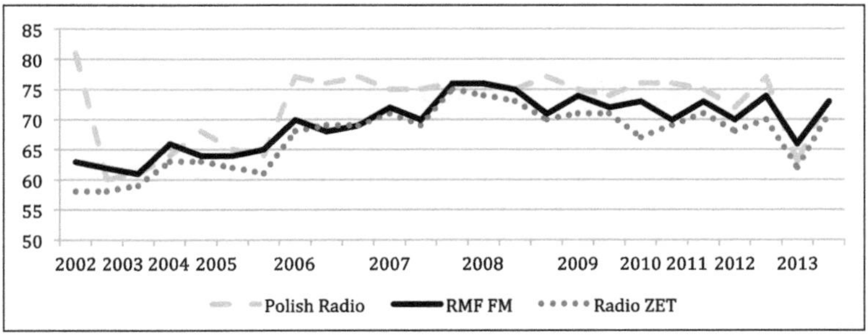

Source: CBOS

Relatively small differences between the stations are confirmed in an analysis of reliability of information programs broadcast by particular television stations[30]. Average assessment of reliability of information programs in the public television, TVN, TVN24, as well as Polsat and Polsat News differ only slightly.

Fig./Tab. 3.9: Assessment of reliability of news programs and current affairs programs

	Average on a scale from 1 to 5[31]	Standard deviation	N
TVP1, TVP2, TVP Info	3.61	1.12	913
TVN and TVN 24	3.60	1.21	853
Polsat and Polsat News	3.57	1.12	829

Source: CBOS

3.2.3 DAP expert opinions on the quality of information

General expert assessment of the quality of information on the public sphere is negative.

30 Based on survey conducted from October 4th to 10th 2012 on random sample of adult Poles, N=1007. M. Omyła-Rudzka, *Assessment of reliability of news programs and current affairs programs.*

31 Average answers on a scale from 1 to 5, where 1: completely unreliable, 5: completely reliable.

Both the public and private media provide poor information. Experts mentioned the deterioration of quality caused by tabloidization, i.e. the replacement of reliable journalism (including the investigative journalism) by sensational news (so-called infotainment).

Fig./Tab. 3.10: The level of information on public institutions

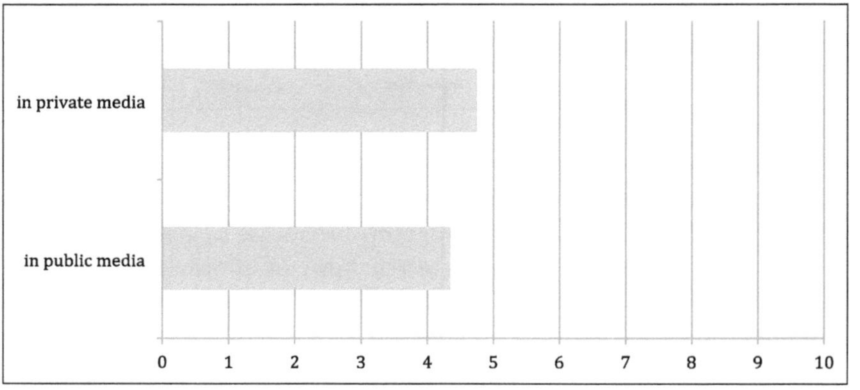

Source: DAP expert survey. Average on a scale from 0 to 10

Specialists prepared detailed assessment of the three sources of information that the majority of the Polish society watch or listen to and that most often serve as a source of information on the public sphere. They are TVP and PR (jointly), TVN and TVN24, and Polsat.

Fig./Tab. 3.11: Accuracy of information on public matters

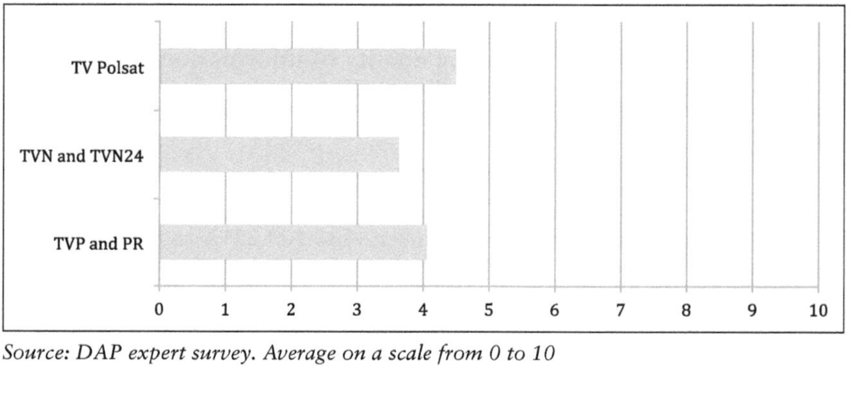

Source: DAP expert survey. Average on a scale from 0 to 10

All the three media, both the public and the private, receive relatively low notes in terms of completeness and accuracy of information. Polsat stands out with regards to objectivity as the station received significantly better notes than the others.

Fig./Tab 3.12: Objectivity of information on public matters

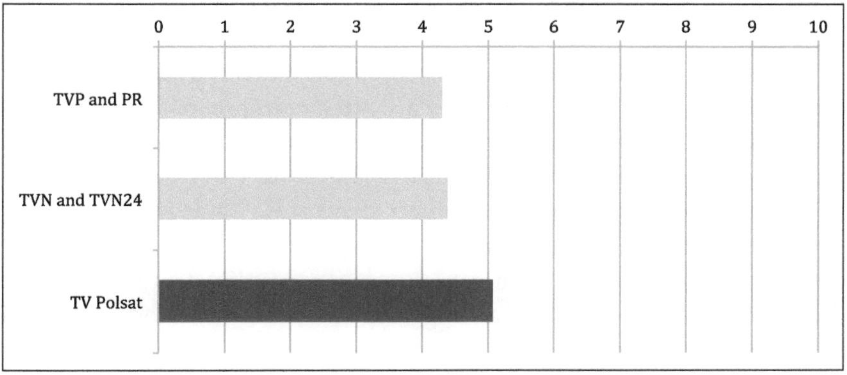

Source: DAP expert survey. Average on a scale from 0 to 10

3.3 Ownership of the media

According to the results of a study entitled Media and Democracy in Central and Eastern Europe (MDCEE), which was conducted between 2010 and 2013 by Oxford University, "general assessment of freedom and pluralism of the media in Poland is positive."[32]

One of the indicated threats is the politicisation of the media or their "colonization" by political parties. In the case of Poland it especially concerns the public media. Another noneconomic factor restricting freedom of speech is legal protection of religious feelings.

An important factor that shapes the situation of the media in the region is linked to the economic transformations. Some tendencies are global,

32 P. Bajomi-Lazar, H. Örnebring, V. Štětka, *Poland. A country report for the ERC-funded project on Media and Democracy in Central and Eastern Europe*, 2011, p. 24 [online]. Available online on: http://mde.politics.ox.ac.uk/index.php/country-reports (accessed on 11.16.2013).

while others are typical for the region. One of the interesting phenomena of recent years is a change in the ownership structure of the mass media in the region. Since the outbreak of the crisis in 2008, multinationals on the media market in the majority of Central and Eastern Europe have been losing their significance. It has been called de-Westernisation of the ownership in the media[33]. These processes have affected Poland as well: News Corporation has withdrawn, while Mecom and Axel Springer have limited their operation.

The place vacated by corporations in almost all countries of the region is taken by local press tycoons. They are often entrepreneurs operating in several sectors. This situation spells danger: "mainstream media organizations are increasingly facing the risk of getting woven into the local political-economic networks and power structures. While [press tycoons] can indeed provide a temporary sanctuary for part of the journalistic community and perhaps even save some news outlets from extinction, the price to be paid for this arrangement might well be too high both for the media, who are putting their autonomy at stake and getting instrumentalized for hidden business/political interests, as well as for democracy, which is widely believed to rely on independent and genuinely pluralistic media."[34]

Against other countries, Poland looks quite positive as the role of press tycoons is relatively insignificant and there are no individuals with criminal record among them, as it happens to be in other countries[35].

3.4 Professionalization of journalism and accountability of the media

The level of professionalism among journalists raises many concerns. Both competence and reliability of journalists informing on the public sphere is rated below the middle point of the scale.

33 V. Stetka, *From Multinationals to Business Tycoons: Journalistic Autonomy in Central and Eastern Europe*, "The International Journal of Press/Politics" 2012, XX(X), p. 1–24.

34 Ibid, p. 19.

35 Ibid, p. 16.

Fig./Tab. 3.13: Assessment of professional preparation of journalists

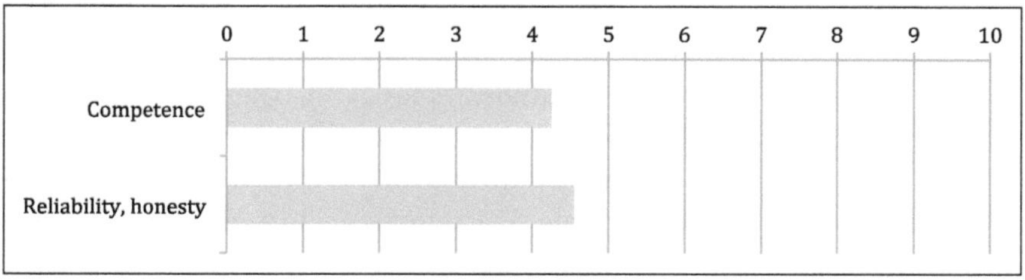

Source: DAP expert survey. Average on a scale from 0 to 10

In case of incorrect information in the media, irreparable damage to the citizen's reputation might occur. It is difficult to correct this information and the possibility to do so is assessed negatively.

Fig./Tab. 3.14: Assessment of the possibility of successful correction of incorrect information by individuals and institutions adversely affected by the media

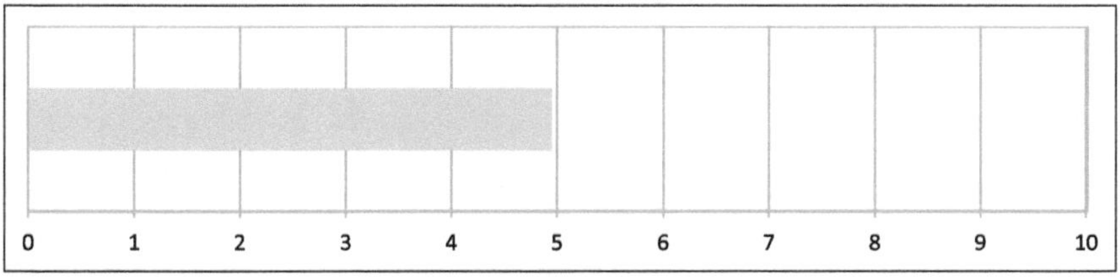

Source: DAP expert survey. Average on a scale from 0 to 10

3.5 Local press

Printed and electronic media operating at the level of communes and counties constitute a locally significant source of information. The period of the political transformation initiated dynamic growth of intensity of their operation. Nevertheless, they struggle with similar problems as regional and national titles, and additionally with problems resulting from the small scale of their operation.

The state of the local press was analyzed by the Bureau of Research of the Polish Sejm (Pokrzycka 2013). Its report concludes that the market of local press is very rich, diversified, and unstable. Generally speaking, every second press title is published locally (there are 2.5-3 thousand of them), but the vast majority have a circulation not exceeding 2,000. The instability of local newspapers is seen in frequent bankruptcies and the emergence of new press titles. Newspapers and magazines were most often published by private owners (39%) and local authorities (36.5%). There is no complete data regarding readership. However, available studies demonstrate growth.

Local press has an informative and controlling role, hence its popularity. It is, however, very susceptible to economic factors and local government pressure.

Newspaper problems have their source in financial difficulties of local publishers. Difficult situation very often impacts proper fulfilling of the control mission. Dependence on various financial sources might lead to their self-censorship and bias.

Pressure exerted by local authorities, businesses or entrepreneurs might also lead to pathologies. Public officials often try to control published materials. The study states that critical comments presented in newspapers might lead to further difficulties in obtaining information and intimidation due to litigation and financial penalties. In case of civil disputes journalists are sometimes left on their own by the editors.

3.6 Summary

Various sources of information on the mass media used in the analyses generally lead to similar conclusions: the media in Poland are free and they ensure access to information on the public sphere, even though the level and objectivity of information in many cases raises doubts.

Assessment of the media should be contextualized; evaluation assumes adopting a reference point. If this point is the state of the media in countries of similar political and economic situation (EU member states from Central and Eastern Europe or, more widely, OECD states) the conclusions are moderately optimistic. With regard to the quality of the media, Poland is in the middle of the ranking of the developed countries and above its midpoint for the countries of the region. This consensus is reflected in the Polish public opinion. Both the general rating of the largest broadcasters and assessment of the quality and neutrality of the information is positive.

Similarly to other countries of the region, and in the developed world in general, the media are getting weaker economically. Neutrality and objectivity of information published by privately-owned newspapers, radio and television stations is at risk of being subjected to business considerations. As circulation and advertising revenues fall, media corporations rely on other sources of income, which results in conflict of interests. Moreover, information is increasingly commercialized: entertainment replaces substantive news and analysis. The public media are not immune to market trends. Their quality is at risk owing to decreasing revenue from the audiovisual licence fees.

Deterioration of the economic position of print media, TV and radio has negative impact on the professional community. The position of journalists is fairly weak; media employees are often underpaid and they increasingly work without a permanent contract. As a result, the quality of journalism decreases: experienced and well-paid professionals are replaced with low-paid and inexperienced personnel.

Bibliography

P. Bajomi-Lazar, H. Örnebring, V. Stetka, *Poland. A country report for the ERC-funded project on Media and Democracy in Central and Eastern Europe* [online]. Available online on: http://mde.politics.ox.ac.uk/index.php/country-reports (accessed on 11.16.2013).

Freedom of the Press 2013 [online]. Available online on: http://www.freedomhouse.org/report-types/freedom-press (accessed on 01.16.2014).

M. Omyła-Rudzka, Ocena wiarygodności programów informacyjnych i publicystycznych. [Assessment of reliability of news programs and current affairs programs]. A report by CBOS [online]. Available online on: http://www.cbos.pl/SPISKOM.POL/2012/K_150_12.PDF; (accessed on 04.02.2013).

Press Freedom Index 2013 [online].Available online on: http://en.rsf.org/spip.php?page=classement&id_rubrique=1054 (accessed 11.20.2013).

L. Pokrzycka, *Kondycja prasy lokalnej w Polsce* [State of Local Press in Poland], Biuro Analiz Sejmowych – Infos, No.6(143), p. 1–4.

V. Stetka, *From Multinationals to Business Tycoons: Journalistic Autonomy in Central and Eastern Europe*, "The International Journal of Press/Politics" 2013, XX(X), p. 1–24.

Sustainable Governance Indicators [online]. Available online on: http://www.sgi-network.org/index.php (accessed on 01.16.2014).

4. Corruption

Both international organizations dealing with corruption and public opinion agree with the statement that corruption poses a threat to "rule of law, democracy and human rights, undermines good governance, fairness and social justice, distorts competition, hinders economic development and endangers the stability of democratic institutions and the moral foundations of society."[36] Additionally, it is a phenomenon that is difficult to measure since "everyone knows it exists but few admit they have directly encountered it. It is difficult to estimate the dimensions of this phenomenon which is accompanied by elusiveness, changeability, lack of witnesses, traces, and revealed victims" (*A Supreme Audit Office Report for 2012,* henceforth as NIK 2012). Nevertheless, corruption is the subject of numerous studies, conducted both by domestic and international organizations.

In this report we discuss legal conditions and corruption cases: the areas threatened by corruption, undertaken anti-corruption actions and their effectiveness. We also present DAP experts' and society opinions on the phenomenon of corruption, as well as four significant international measures of corruption: the *Corruption Perceptions Index* by Transparency International and corruption measures from the *Rule of Law Index* in the World Justice Project and *Sustainable Governance Index* created by the Bertelsmann Foundation and the Index of Corruption Control by the World Bank.

In the second part of the chapter we deal with the phenomenon of lobbying in Poland. Putting lobbying beside corruption in one chapter might not be most accurate as it suggests that lobbying is as a rule, wrong. However, from the point of view of democratic control of regulations and practices, limiting the corruption-generating nature of this phenomenon is significant.

36 Preamble to the Criminal Law Convention on Corruption on corruption signed by Poland in Strasbourg on 01.27.1998.

4.1 Corrupt behaviour on the central and local levels

4.1.1 Legal environment

A range of domestic and international legal acts, including EU regulations (an overview of legal acts from *Polish legal provisions* 2014[37]) aim to prevent the phenomenon of corruption in Poland.

Among Polish domestic legislation, the key document containing regulations on corruption is the Penal Code (PC), wherein the crimes of corruption and their subjects in the public sector are detailed (Art.228-231of PC) – including also electoral corruption (Art.250a of PC) and economic corruption (Art. 269a, 269b and 302 of PC). The Penal Code also defines punishment for committed corruption offences. The bill on the Central Anti-Corruption Bureau (*Ustawa o Centralnym Biurze Antykorupcyjnym*) from 9 June 2006 is of no less importance. It created an institution specializing in tracking down corruption offences and it contains the first unified official definition of corruption; it also thoroughly describes the actions and behaviours that contain elements of corruption.

Apart from the two abovementioned legal acts, the phenomenon of corruption is also regulated by a range of bills, internal regulations of the Sejm and Senate of the Republic of Poland, rules creating an obligation for public figures to submit a declaration of financial interests as well as regulations governing specific behaviour and good practices.

Poland is also bound by international agreements and conventions, which regulate the rules regarding corruption on the domestic and international levels. Poland joined the Convention on Combating Bribery of Foreign Public Officials in International Trade Transactions, adopted in 1997 by the OECD. In 2002, Poland ratified two conventions of the Council of Europe: the Criminal Law Convention on Corruption and the Civil Law Convention on Corruption and in this way joined GRECO (Group of States against corruption), an anti-corruption agency of the Council of Europe.

In 2006 the UN Convention on corruption was ratified. The European Union also has significant influence on the policy of member states in

37 A detailed description of legal conditions for corruption might be found in Celina Nowak's *Corruption in Polish Criminal Law Against International Regulations*. Beck: 2008.

terms of combating corruption as it regulates matters related to this issue with convention[38], framework decisions, protocols and regulations.

4.1.2 Corruption cases

Corruption in Poland

Public opinion around the world perceives corruption as a problem, although particular countries differ when we discuss how significant this phenomenon is. Among EU member state societies the Greeks, the Portuguese, the Cypriots, and the Hungarians attach the greatest importance to it (*Eurobarometer* No. 374, 2012).

The lowest percentage of citizens who believe corruption is a serious problem was noted in Denmark. Otherwise, in the Netherlands, Finland and Sweden the percentage of respondents who disagree with the statement that corruption constitutes a serious problem exceeded the percentage of affirmative responses. Poland took the seventh position in this rank, slightly below the average for the Union (Figure 4.1).

Fig./Tab. 4.1: Is corruption a serious problem in your country?

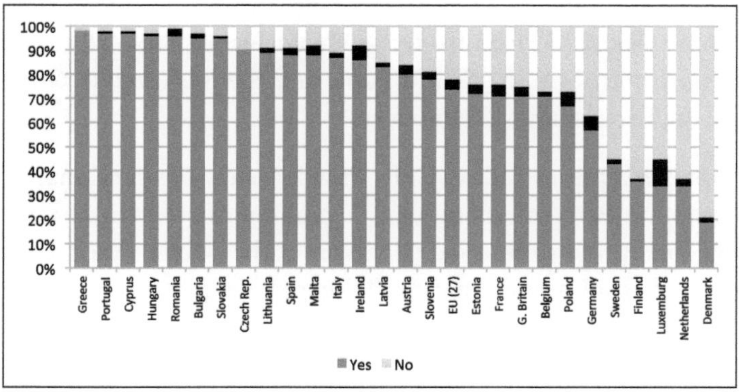

Source: Eurobarometer 2012

38 Convention on the protection of the European Communities' financial interests (07.26.1995); Convention drawn up on the basis of Article K.3 (2) (c) of the Treaty on European Union on the fight against corruption involving officials of the European Communities or officials of Member States of the European Union, Convention of the Council of Europe on Laundering, Search, Seizure and Confiscation of the Proceeds from Crime and on the Financing of Terrorism.

Studies conducted in Poland[39] also demonstrate that the vast majority of citizens believe that corruption is a serious problem (40% of the respondents are convinced that it is a very serious problem, 43% believe it is a rather serious problem, 9% believe that this phenomenon is rather an insignificant problem, while 1% believe it is a very small problem). This conviction held by the majority has been slightly changing over time but in recent years it has shown a downward trend (Feliksiak 2013).

Domestic DAP experts are also convinced that Poland is not entirely free from corruption; the experts are not very positive about the real effectiveness of actions undertaken to combat the problem. In terms of freedom from corruption, the national administration, with an average score of 5.74, is perceived better than the local authority, which is placed slightly above the average.

International indicators

The image of Poland in the eyes of international organizations dealing with corruption is much more positive. Below we discuss an assessment of Poland by the four significant measures relevant to this issue: the Corruption Perceptions Index by Transparency International, indicators from the *Rule of Law* report (derived from the World Justice Project), the Index of Corruption Control by the World Bank and the *Sustainable Governance Index* by the Bertelsmann Foundation.

Corruption Perceptions Index (CPI), Transparency International 2013
The Corruption Perceptions Index is a ranking of countries based on the perceived corruption-generating character of the public sector, with scores being derived from a combination of surveys, expert opinions, and estimates on corruption.

According to data from Transparency International, in 2013, Poland, with a CPI index of 60 (the higher the index value, the less corruption there is), was located at the 38th position out of 175 countries that were ranked in the study overall while also occupying the second position among the post-communist democracies of Central and Eastern Europe

39 A study called *Current Problems and Affairs* (277), June 6–12 2013 - a representative sample of adult inhabitants of Poland (N=1010).

(behind Estonia). It's worth mentioning that for only 23% of the EU member states (including Switzerland, Norway, and Iceland) was the CPI index value above 80 (no risk of corruption).

An analysis of the trend shows that the problem of corruption in Poland has been gradually decreasing since 2005. The time has come for a methodological remark: until 2011 the Corruption Perceptions Index was measured on an eleven-point scale from 0 to 10; and since 2012 a scale from 0 to 100 has been in use (in a figure the data for 2001-2011 was calculated in a way that allows unification with the latest results). Moreover, in 2012 the methodology of creating the index also changed, which results in a collapse of the time series. Nevertheless, even the data from 2000 – 2010 demonstrates significant improvement in assessing the anti-corruption policy in Poland.

World Justice Project – Rule of Law Index (2012)[40]

Another source of data on global corruption is the World Justice Project, which deals with studying the rule of law in 97 countries. According to a ranking done by the World Justice Project, Poland, with the result of 0.72 occupies the 27th position among 97 analyzed countries in terms of lack of corruption in public institutions. As a country included in the group of countries with high income, it occupies the 23rd place out of 30, and among the countries of the region included in this group, Estonia and Hungary occupy a higher position.

Corruption Control Index – World Bank[41]

The level of corruption control constitutes one of the six indicators listed in the study named "Worldwide Governance Indicators", which was developed by the World Bank. According to this index, in 2012 the value for the Index of Corruption Control in Poland was 0.59 (on a scale from –2.5 to 2.5). This value places Poland slightly above the average for OECD countries within the upper income quartile (the group in which Poland is included). It is worth mentioning that since 2006 the value of the index

---

40 http://worldjusticeproject.org/sites/default/files/WJP_Index_Report_2012.pdf

41 http://info.worldbank.org/governance/wgi/index.aspx#reports

has been systematically increasing, which means that the state of corruption control in Poland is increasing. Only Estonia has a higher index value among the countries of the region.

Sustainable Governance Index 2011

Assessing corruption is also the objective of a project called the Sustainable Governance Index, developed by the Bertelsmann Foundation. In terms of preventing corruption (the qualitative index based on expert opinions), Poland received 6 points (out of 10)[42], which means that most mechanisms which guarantee honesty are efficient and hence discourage irregularities.

Despite relatively positive assessments of anti-corruption mechanisms, experts believe that some signs of corruption, e.g. bribery, constitute a problem in Poland.

The level of corruption control in the SGI report is measured in terms of quantity, on the basis of indicators developed by the World Bank (in the case of SGI 2011 it was data from 2009). The index created in this way situated Poland at the 26th position, with an index value of 3.22 (on a scale from 0 to 10).

Areas threatened by corruption

The complexity of the character of corruption and the lack of a unified definition make it very difficult to investigate what areas are most threatened by corruption; likewise it is not easy to estimate its real range.

One of the sources showing the range of corruption (and the effectiveness of various institutions in combating it) is the *Corruption Map*, which contains data regarding corruption offences committed in particular years[43]. In 2012 the most often registered offences include venality of a public official (Art. 228 PC), bribery (Art. 229 PC), and abuse of powers

42 In the study entitled *Transformation Index* conducted also by the Bertelsmann Foundation in the *prosecution of office abuse* index, Poland received an 8 (10 is the highest note), which means that it performs relatively well compared to new democracies.

43 These are corruption offences recorded by the Police, Internal Security Agency (ABW), Central Anti-Corruption Bureau (CBA), Prosecutor's office, border patrol, and military Police in the files of the National Criminal Register.

of a public official (Art. 231 §2 PC). The most rare cases detected are those concerning corruption in sport. The highest number of corruption offences is attributed to the most numerous law enforcement authorities: the police.

The most common signs of corruption enumerated by DAP experts are the following: bid and contest rigging (e.g. through introducing criteria or legal limitations to eliminate certain bidders), supporting businesses with connections to politicians, nepotism. Expert opinions are confirmed in the data we collected.

A NIK report from 2012 points out that the most corruption-generating zone is local administration: every fourth investigation conducted relates to this area. In comparison, 16% of proceedings concern the economy section, 10% local administrative bodies, 8% customs administration, 7% EU programs, 6% law enforcement and judiciary as well as public health services and pharmacy, 5% armed forces, 4% tax authorities and state aims, 3% sport (NIK 2012).

Fig./Tab. 4.2: In which of the fields presented do you think corruption is encountered most often?

	2000	2001	2003	2004	2005	2006	2009	2010	2013
Among politicians– party activists, councillors, MPs, senators	54%	52%	60%	61%	35%	44%	55%	60%	62%
In the health service	47%	42%	43%	50%	53%	58%	54%	58%	53%
In commune, county, voivodeship offices	29%	25%	29%	21%	28%	25%	28%	31%	27%
In police	31%	23%	25%	34%	31%	28%	16%	15%	21%
In central offices and ministries	38%	29%	37%	34%	22%	32%	27%	26%	18%
In national companies	13%	12%	11%	11%	9%	15%	14%	13%	13%
In companies	13%	9%	11%	12%	8%	9%	10%	8%	9%
In education	7%	8%	4%	4%	8%	3%	3%	3%	3%

	2000	2001	2003	2004	2005	2006	2009	2010	2013
In banks	6%	3%	5%	4%	3%	2%	4%	3%	2%
Somewhere else	1%	0%	1%	1%	2%	0%	4%	1%	2%
Hard to say	1%	12%	8%	6%	15%	10%	8%	7%	8%

Source: Feliksiak 2013

According to public opinion, corruption does not concern ordinary citizen and remains the competence of politicians: party activists, councillors, MPs and senators (62%). Over a half of those questioned (53%) believe that the health service is threatened by corruption. In both cases in recent years there has been growth in the number of respondents convinced about the corrupt character of these institutions (Feliksiak 2013).

According to the respondents, corruption among public officials and politicians means first of all nepotism, but also favouritism. Almost a half of those questioned (47%) believe that it is a very common practice to fill the posts in offices, companies, banks, etc. with relatives and friends; 32% mention arranging contracts, government orders for family and friends with private businesses.

Fig./Tab. 4.3: Frequency of various signs of corruption among civil servants and politicians

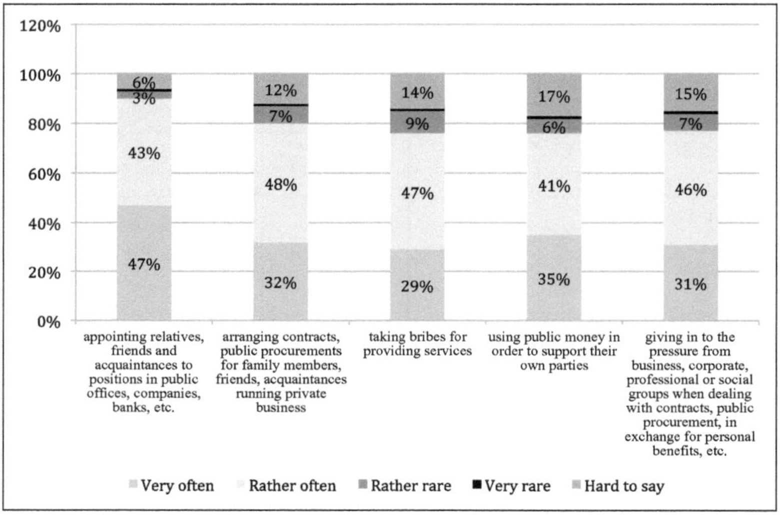

Source: Feliksiak 2013

Combating corruption

Poles negatively assess anti-corruption actions taken by the government; they are not convinced that there is the political will to combat this phenomenon either (Feliksiak 2013). Only every third Pole believes that such a will exists (4% definitely yes, 27% probably yes). The percentage of the respondents who agree with this statement has dropped drastically in the last three years (in 2010 56% of the respondents noticed a political will to combat corruption).

Assessments of the current government operations in combating corruption are also getting worse. Only 15% of the respondents assess the anti-corruption operations of the authorities as good or very good (in 2010 it was 38%). Moreover, the percentage of the respondents who assess this aspect of government activity as very bad has significantly increased (in 2010 it was 8%, and in 2013 it increased to 21% - Feliksiak 2013).

Negative assessments of government activity might be caused by the fact that it is extremely hard to demonstrate the effectiveness of measures applied for combating corruption. First of all, the method of collecting the data by various institutions[44] is not standardized, which is why the data collected about the issue differs. Secondly, the collected data is of little value in terms of estimating the degree of corruption (Czubek 2013).

Apart from detection and prosecution of corruption offences, a vital element of anti-corruption policy is prevention. Since 2002 Polish authorities have intensified their activity, implementing subsequent anti-corruption programs aiming at making changes in legislation, carrying out information and education campaigns and organizational activity, such as introducing ISO certificates, anti-corruption procedures, a codes of ethics, the institution of the ethical advisor. The program evaluation revealed numerous irregularities and excessive optimism in terms of implementing the targets. The main problem turned out to be the lack of coherent anti-corruption policy followed by discretion of the number and type of implemented solutions, unstable and too vague legal regulations, as well

44 In Poland there are numerous registries of offences of corrupt nature run by the National Criminal Register (KCIK), Police Crime Statistics System TEMIDA, Central Anti-Corruption Bureau (CBA) and Internal Security Agency (ABW) databases, National Criminal Records.

as a lack of systematic and permanent monitoring of procedures (Kubiak, Krzewińska 2011).

Despite the successes of anti-corruption measures undertaken in Poland and recorded by international organizations, corruption is not a phenomenon that can be fully eliminated. This is influenced by changing circumstances (social changes, norm and value changes, new trends in the economy or new tasks awaiting a modern state), which bring about new challenges for governments (anti-corruption tools in Poland). The Polish authorities are also persistent in their struggle with corruption.

4.2 Transparency of relations between politics and the economy

Lobbying in Poland is perceived by public opinion as a definitely negative phenomenon. It is accompanied by a low level of knowledge about lobbying as such, as well as the legal conditions regulating it.

As CBOS studies show, a significant percentage of the respondents (57%) condemn lobbying and agree with the statement that it is a negative phenomenon, which facilitates corruption and abuse. Only 25% believe that it is a positive phenomenon allowing people to present their arguments to the officials (18% have no opinion on the matter). It is worth noticing that as many as 45% of the respondents never came across the term "lobbying," while 65% never heard of legal regulations for lobbying activity. Despite a lack of knowledge, as many as 47% of Poles are convinced that the influence of lobbyists on the law-making process in Poland is significant (very big according to 11%, while according to 6% rather big). 23% of the respondents state that this influence is minimal. 30% of the respondents have no opinion on the matter (Kowalczuk 2013).

Despite the fact that Poles most often associate lobbying with corruption, it is an indispensable element of democracy, facilitating its practice for social or professional groups, which are thereby able to influence individuals who make decisions in the country. Lobbying does not only mean influencing decision-makers over large concerns. Lobbyists (going beyond the legal definition) might include all types of interest groups as broad lobbying activity is rooted in democratic freedom of association, right to representation, access to public information etc., whereas a low assessment of lobbying might result from a law-making system of little transparency:

citizens do not know who influences decision makers and what they want to gain from it.

4.2.1 Legal conditions

In Polish law lobbying activity is regulated by a bill on lobbying activity in the law-making process (*Ustawa o działalności lobbingowej w procesie stanowienia prawa*), passed on 7 July 2005. This bill defines the phenomenon and specifies the rules of disclosure for lobbying activity in the law-making process, the rules of pursuing professional lobbying activity, forms of professional control of professional lobbying activity and the rules for keeping the register of entities dealing with professional lobbying activity.

This bill has been criticized for a lack of sufficient regulations concerning lobbying activity (Jasiecki 2005). The main criticism concerned the limited range of the bill: the rules concern only individuals who perform lobbying activity professionally – a group which *de facto* constitutes a small percentage of lobbyists[45] (as of 5 January 2014 on the Sejm websites only 81 lobbyists were registered[46]). Entities not covered by the bill might conduct unlimited lobbying activity, which suggests that the bill is an insufficient solution for preventing unfair lobbying. However, additional solutions are being gradually implemented which are to prevent the formation of pathology (e.g. introduction of the rules of contact with potential lobbyists such as business representatives in central offices, while individuals participating in the Sejm committees are required to provide information on their company, etc.). Transparency in the lobbying process is also increasing: for instance ministry websites post submitted points,

45 Other entities dealing with lobbying in Poland include employer organisations, individual entrepreneurs, lobbying specialists employed by big corporations, employee organizations, churches and religious communities, associations and organizations of economic self-government, as well as other NGOs, which, within the meaning of the bill, are not considered professional lobbyists.

46 A list of the Sejm-registered lobbyists covers only individuals who are in the possession of a current Sejm pass. There is no data on lobbyists who finished work on projects from different bills. Annual reports containing information on actions undertaken in the Sejm by entities of a professional lobbying profile are submitted with a long delay (as of January 2014, the data available was coming from as long ago as early 2010).

their authors' details and the decision either accepting or rejecting the points. Also, organizations which are not covered by the bill nevertheless take care to ensure the transparency of their activity.

The provisions of the bill concern predominantly legislation on the central level (the Sejm of the Republic of Poland, ministries) but they do not concern lobbying on the local, voivodeship level, which is regulated only by provisions included in the voivodeship statutes, as well as in the procedural rules of the council and Marshall's Office, which regulate the contacts of interested entities with voivodeship council bodies (Zbieranek 2010).

4.2.2 Cases of unfair lobbying

In Poland interest groups unequal in terms of influence are struggling to maximize their own benefits often at the cost of other groups or the whole of society. When it comes to domestic companies, both their level of organization as interest groups and their real influence on public decisions is diverse.

Large private companies are relatively well organized; on the one hand they form professional clubs, confederations, and other types of organizations, while on the other hand they act on the basis of institutionalized informal, social, direct contacts between representatives of business, administration, and politics, in effect taking advantage of personal ties and the principle of service reciprocity (Jasiecki 2013, p. 252).

Direct connections with party decision makers and the government administration also play a role in the case of a state-owned enterprise (where management has very deep roots in party elites; where a public sphere activity orientation is dominant, and close collaboration with trade unions is often encountered). State-owned enterprises impact politicians to the greatest extent. The foundation of their relations with decision makers – essentially a system of interrelationships between the management of state-owned enterprises and their economic surroundings and politicians – is not transparent enough (Jasiecki 2013, p. 243–244).

It needs to be stressed, however, that the role of personal contacts between the world of the economy and the world of politics is significantly decreasing as a result of growing pressure calling for transparency in relations between the economy and politics, inspired and monitored by organizations and associations of representatives of the business world, as well as legislation changes.

Small and medium-sized companies constitute a group, which has the least impact on political decision makers. They rather focus on reacting to the policy of the authorities and not its initiation or modification. They use first of all collective methods of influence: protests, blockades, petitions, etc.; individual methods (presentations of the company's position or meeting with decision makers) play a significant role only on the local level. The reason for this is first of all a high level of dispersion: small and medium-sized enterprises associate in numerous employer organizations with limited political resources. Fragmentation, a passive style of action and a lack of an expert base mean that the impact they have on public matters and administrative decisions is minimal (Jasiecki 2013, p. 246-257).

Some believe that it is foreign capital owners that benefit from an especially privileged position (often due to favourable privatisation decisions) and that they control some sectors of the economy. It is an influential group of actors who impact administrative and legislative decisions with the help of professional (and costly) forms of pressure. Despite taking on experts and professional lobbyists, their actions might sometimes create powerful pressure that is by its nature corrupt. Furthermore, they might lobby to the detriment of local producers and consumers, which will lead to the lowering of their chances for success in the global economy (Jasiecki 2013).

The limited entity range of the bill regulating lobbying activity prevents effective monitoring of the scale of the phenomenon of unfair lobbying at the local level.

Talks conducted with representatives of the voivodeship government and case studies (Makowski 2010) confirm the existence of lobbying at the level of the voivodeship government, which takes the form of action on the public forum but also attempts to apply pressure in informal situations. Lobbying (conducted within the limits allowed by the law by lower ranking representatives of the local government, NGOs and citizens) is assessed positively. Attempts to exercise influence by entrepreneurs are assessed much worse.

Numerous studies show that the situation in Poland is gradually improving, while standards of relations between the economy and politics are slowly adjusting towards those existing in Western Europe. This situation is influenced, among others, by economic growth, the integration process with the European Union, the necessity of adjusting the law to international standards, the increased effectiveness of the state apparatus and social pressure on executing the rule of transparency (Kobylińska and others 2012). It is still necessary to introduce regulations on the local level.

4.3 Summary

The assessment of corruption in Poland is not uniform. The vast majority of citizens believe that corruption in the Polish public sphere constitutes a serious problem while both the methods and willingness to combat it are insufficient. On the other hand, international organizations studying the issue of corruption give Poland a positive assessment. One of the more significant indicators, the Corruption Perceptions Index, includes Poland in the group of countries, which are not threatened by corruption. DAP experts also have a relatively positive opinion; their assessment is closest to the statement that corruption in Poland exists but is not common.

The thesis that the risk of corruption in Poland is decreasing might be supported by changes in how corruption is being studied by organizations dealing with this issue (e.g. Batory Foundation shifted the topic of studies from corruption towards good governance). It needs to be noted, however, that in spite of visible changes at the macro-level (ministry, government) various signs of corruption (e.g. nepotism) have been a grave problem at the local level for some time now. The experts also believe that it is necessary to improve the implementation of government anti-corruption policies.

Bibliography

M.D. Agrast, Juan Carlos Botero, Joel Martinez, Alejandro Ponce, Christine S. Pratt, *The World Justice Project. Rule of Law Index 2012–2013*, Washington D.C.: The World Justice Project 2013. Available online on: http://worldjusticeproject.org/sites/default/files/WJP_Index_Report_2012.pdf (accessed on 12.20.2013).

Corruption Perception Index 2013, [online]. Available online on: http://www.transparency.org/cpi2013/results (accessed on 01.15.2014).

G. Czubek, *Polityka antykorupcyjna* [Anti-corruption Policy], in: *Raport otwarcia Koalicji na rzecz Otwartego Rządu* [A Report on Opening Coalition for Open Government], Warsaw: the Batory Foundation, 2013.

Special Eurobarometer No. 374: *Corruption*, 2012 [online]. Available online on: http://ec.europa.eu/public_opinion/archives/ebs/ebs_374_en.pdf (accessed on 01.07.2014).

M. Feliksiak, *Opinie o korupcji w Polsce* [Opinions on Corruption in Poland], CBOS, Warsaw 2013. Available online on: http://www.cbos.pl/SPISKOM.POL/2013/K_105_13.PDF (accessed on 10.11.2013).

K. Jasiecki, *Kapitalizm po polsku. Między modernizacją a peryferiami Unii Europejskiej* [Capitalism in Polish. Between modernization and the periphery of the European Union], Warsaw: IFIS PAN, 2013.

Idem, *Lobbing po polsku* [Lobbying in Polish]. "Biuletyn Dialogu Społecznego" no. 9, 2005, p. 5–7.

Mechanizmy przeciwdziałania korupcji w Polsce, Raport z Monitoringu [Anti-corruption Measures in Poland, A Report on Monitoring], edited by A. Kobylińska, G. Makowski, M. Solon-Lipiński, ISP, Warsaw 2012.

K. Kowalczuk, *Konflikty interesów i lobbing – dylematy polityków* [Conflict of interests and lobbying – politicians' dilemmas], CBOS, Warsaw 2013. Available online on: http://www.cbos.pl/SPISKOM.POL/2013/K_122_13.PDF (accessed on 11.10.2013).

A. Kubiak, A. Krzewińska, *Raport z badań nad skutecznością wdrażania strategii antykorupcyjnych rządów RP w wybranych instytucjach centralnych w latach 2007–2011* [A Report on Studies of Effectiveness of Implementing Anti-corruption Strategies of Polish Governments in Selected Central Institutions from 2007 to 2011], in: *Polityka antykorupcyjna. Ocena skuteczności polityki antykorupcyjnej polskich rządów prowadzonej w latach 2001–2011* [Anti-corruption Policy. Assessment of Effectiveness of Anti-corruption Policy of Polish Governments from 2001 to 2011], Batory Foundation, Warsaw 2011.

Lobbing w samorządzie województwa. Raport z badań i monitoringu [Lobbying in the Voivodeship Government. A Report of Studies and Monitoring], edited by G. Makowski, Warsaw: ISP, 2011.

Mapa Korupcji. Stan przestępczości korupcyjnej w Polsce w 2012 r. [Corruption Map. State of Corruption Crime in Poland in 2012 r.], Warsaw 2013. Available online on: http://www.antykorupcja.gov.pl/ftp/filmy/Mapa%20korupcji%202013.pdf (accessed on 02.15.2014).

C. Matthes, R. Markowski, F. Bönker, *Sustainable Governance Indicators 2011. Poland Report*, 2011. Available online on: http://www.sgi-network.org/pdf/SGI11_Poland.pdf (accessed on 01.15.2014).

M. Omyła-Rudzka, *Stosunek do łapownictwa i doświadczenia z nim związane* [Approach to Bribery and Experiences Connected to it], CBOS, Warsaw 2013. Available online on: http://www.cbos.pl/SPISKOM.POL/2013/K_109_13.PDF (accessed on: 10.11. 2013).

Polskie przepisy prawa. Stan prawny na dzień 20.01.2014 [Polish Legal Provisions. Legal state as of 01.20.2014]. Available online on: http://www.antykorupcja.gov.pl/ (accessed on 01.20.2014).

Przewidywane zagrożenia korupcyjne [Anticipated Corruption Risks], CBA, Warsaw 2013. Available online on: http://www.cba.gov.pl (accessed on 01.02 2014).

Raport z działalności Agencji Bezpieczeństwa Wewnętrznego w 2012 r. [A Report on Internal Security Agency Activity in 2012], ABW, Warsaw. Available online on: http://www.abw.gov.pl/ (accessed on 12. 29. 2013).

Raport z działalności NIK za rok 2012 [A Report on Supreme Audit Office Activity for 2012]. Available online on: http://www.nik.gov.pl/plik/id,5017.pdf (accessed on 01.02.2014).

Polityka antykorupcyjna. Ocena skuteczności polityki antykorupcyjnej polskich rządów prowadzonej w latach 2001–2011 [Anti-corruption Policy. Assessment of Effectiveness of Anti-corruption Policy of Polish Governments conducted from 2001 to 2011], edited by J. Winczorek, the Batory Foundation, Warsaw 2013.

Praktyczny przewodnik po lobbingu w samorządzie wojewódzkim [Practical Guide to Lobbying in the Voivodeship Government], edited by J. Zbieranek, ISP, Warsaw.

5. Administration

Even though the functioning of the national administration seems to matter a lot when looking at the quality of a democracy, it is still difficult to find synthetic indicators assessing this field. On the one hand, the existing data is mostly dispersed and it concerns a narrow range in terms of theme or geography. On the other hand, the approach of public opinion towards administration is relatively well-researched.

In this chapter we analyze selected data regarding the functioning of administration in Poland. These studies are enriched with expert as well as regular citizens' opinions.

5.1 Monopoly on using violence (existence of non-state power entities - organized crime groups, informal local networks)

Lack of a state monopoly on the use of violence seems not to be a serious problem in Poland. Detection and limiting the activity of criminal groups is still growing (according to the data of the Central Bureau of Investigation of the Police Headquarters in 2011, the Bureau investigated 595 domestic and international criminal groups; in 2012 this number rose to 772, as in: A Report on Central Bureau of Investigation Activity of Police Headquarters for 2012, henceforth as CBŚ 2012)[47].

There is no data on the existence of informal local networks, their number or type of activity. Relations between criminal structures and local authorities are worrying. Studies show that in 2012 almost half (45%) of the questioned key witnesses (criminals cooperating with the police)[48] assessed

47 This number does not seem small; however, we mean relatively small criminal groups. In 2012 the Central Investigation Bureau (CBŚ) was interested in 156 leaders and 1517 members of organized criminal groups (CBŚ 2012).

48 Witnesses were asked to answer the question "whether, to their knowledge that they acquired when working in the organized criminal group, the group bosses influence functioning of the local authority level: local government, municipality – mayors, presidents". If the answer was affirmative, they were also requested to specify the range of this influence.

the influence of criminal groups' bosses on local authorities' activity as very big or big. This percentage is however lower than in previous years.

It is predominantly police officers and border guards who are subject to the influence of the criminal groups' bosses, with the third largest group vulnerable to their sway being officials of local authority bodies. It is worth mentioning that the percentage of recorded cases involving the influencing of local authority officials in 2012 drastically increased (Rau 2013).

5.2 Ability to collect taxes

A measure of the effectiveness of the national administration is its ability to collect taxes. In the report we take into account two measures of this area of state functionality, namely: the effectiveness of tax offices and the size of the gray economy.

5.2.1 Tax Office Effectiveness

The Supreme Audit Office (NIK) determined *(A Report on Supreme Chamber of Control Activity for 2012,* henceforth as NIK 2012a) that the effectiveness of tax offices in Poland is not satisfactory. The main claims are directed at the local administration and concern insufficient tax arrears collection by municipalities and unclear criteria for granting concessions by municipalities, which creates a corruption-generating mechanism. At the same time the Supreme Chamber of Control positively assessed the collection of personal income tax between 2007 and 2009, even though also in this area a range of irregularities has been recorded.

A reliable indicator applied when studying the state's ability to collect taxes might be a proportion of arrears to tax revenue. The data from 2008–2012 (Tab. 5.1 from: Jagliński 2013), similar to the data from the NIK inspection, show that the number of debtors of the Tax Office is growing every year, as well as the proportion of arrears in tax revenue, which, when putting aside other variables, such as the state of the economy or changes in the fiscal law, might indicate a decreasing ability of the tax administration to collect taxes.

Fig./Tab. 5.1: Proportion of arrears to tax revenue between 2008–2012

	2008	2009	2010	2011	2012
Debtors over PLN 1m	4,337	4,419	4,605	5,113	6,024
Arrears	PLN 12,228m	PLN 12,219m	PLN 13,715m	PLN 15,263m	PLN 18,634m
Tax revenue	PLN 205,016m	PLN 194,545m	PLN 199,833m	PLN 221,553m	PLN 224,014m
Proportion of arrears in revenue	5.96%	6.28%	6.86%	6.89%	8.31%

Source: Jagliński 2013

5.2.2 Gray economy

A measure of the effectiveness of the tax administration apparatus is also the size of the so-called "gray economy," understood as the percentage of individuals performing an unregistered job[49].

The data collected by the Polish Central Statistical Office (GUS) (2010) between 1995-2010 shows that the number of individuals admitting doing unregistered work is decreasing (in 1995– 2,199 thousand, 1998– 1,431 thousand, 2004 – 1,317 thousand, 2009– 785 thousand, during the first nine months of 2010– 732 thousand people).

The size of the gray economy in Poland might be assessed with the help of international data (Schneider 2013). In 2013 Poland occupied the 10th position in terms of the size of the gray economy measured as a percentage of GDP, significantly above the average for European countries. It is worth noticing that among the post-communist democracies only the Czech Republic and Slovakia have better results.

49 The Polish Central Statistical Office (GUS) defines unregistered work as "an employed activity without concluding a contract of employment, an order contract, a task contract or any other written contract between the employer and employee, regardless of the property sector (also in case of natural persons and farms) as well as conducting one's own business if financial duties resulting from this activity (e.g. taxes) are not paid)" (GUS 2010, p. 10).

Fig./Tab. 5.2: The gray economy as a percentage of GDP in Europe in 2013

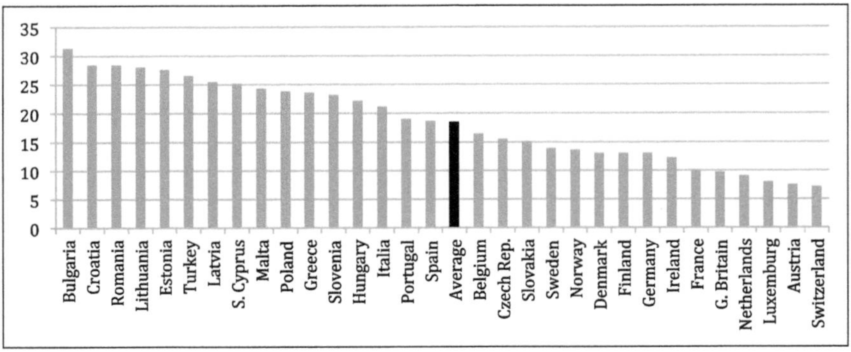

Source: Schneider 2013

The size of the gray economy measured as a percentage of GDP also confirms the information on the decreasing percentage of people working illegally. In table 5.3 we observe a falling trend; however, similar trends are present in all the analyzed European countries. The average size of the gray economy in Europe is however a few percent points lower than in Poland.

Fig./Tab. 5.3: The gray economy as a percentage of GDP between 2003 and 2013

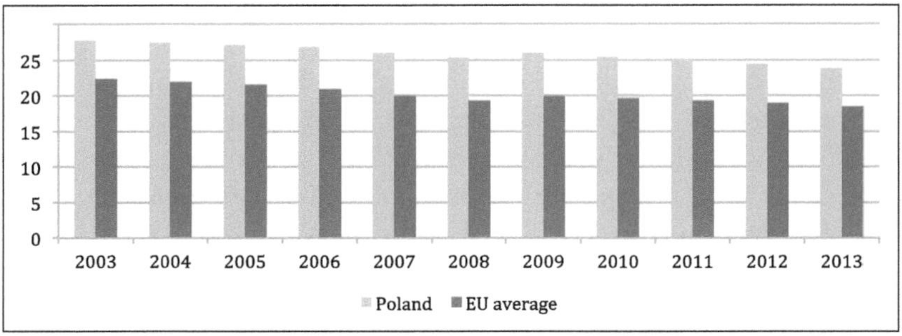

Source: Schneider 2013

5.3 Rationality and neutrality of the administration apparatus (differences in the treatment of various types of citizens)

The rational and neutral activity of the administration is guaranteed by professional official staff whose aim is to professionally, reliably, impartially and politically neutrally execute the state duties[50]. In Poland the rules of its training and functionality are regulated by the Constitution (Articles 60 and 153) and a range of bills[51].

Public officials are recruited in a process guided by the rules of openness, competitiveness, and universality. From the formal point of view it is one's education, qualitifications, and skills that determine whether one is accepted or not, whereas political affiliations, background or gender do not play a role. In order to ensure a professional civil service, in 1990 the National School of Public Administration (KSAP) was established and since then future officials of civil service have been educated there. Apart from that, civil servants employed for the first time in civil service (no graduates of KSAP) are obliged to undergo preparatory practical service.

Despite minor deficiencies in the process of educating and recruiting civil servants, both the competencies and honesty of administration officials are assessed by DAP experts positively, even though the notes are not very high.

It needs to be mentioned, however, that local level officials were deemed as slightly less honest than officials from the central level. The level of competence of both groups is comparable, although the assessment only slightly goes beyond the central point. Experts are rather of the same opinion on these issues. A derogation from observing the principles of civil service recruitment process is political appointment (Heywood and others 2008).

It concerns first of all positions of higher level in the government administration: deputy ministries (this position is formally regarded as political) as well as the position of the director-general, the head of the department, and the deputy head of the department (these positions were re-established as a part of the civil service of higher level in the bill from 2008). As a result of the politicization of positions, there were staff changes following

---

50 Civil Service Code of Ethics from 2002.

51 The bill on civil service (*Ustawa o służbie cywilnej*) from 2008, the bill on government agency officials (*Ustawa o pracownikach urzędów państwowych*) from 1982, the bill on the National School of Public Administration (*Ustawa o Krajowej Szkole Administracji Publicznej*) from 1991, the bill on local government officials (*Ustawa o pracownikach samorządowych*) from 2008.

the change of ministry posts holders, which leads to a break in the continuity of executing tasks. The dependence on the employment of specific persons also influences the personalization of internal relations within an administrative organization.

Additionally, the politically motivated appointment of officials leads to the situation in which they might feel that it is their duty to be loyal towards more than one supervisor, which in turn entails a risk of corruption.

The politicization of official posts constitutes a breaking of the rule on neutrality[52] of administration, which is one of the main rules of ethics of the civil service[53]. This rule means predominantly equal treatment of all citizens, regardless of their political beliefs, sex, religion, or race.

In order to implement the principles of equality before the law, a regulation was included in the Code on Administrative Procedures in 2011. According to the regulation, officials are obliged to keep case sheets. Control over the participation of officials in the decision-making process and transparency of justification for the decisions taken aims at ensuring confidence in administrative bodies' conduct (Łuba 2013).

We did not manage to gain access to the data on the unequal treatment of various citizen groups by the public administration (although the topic of unequal treatment of various citizen groups is being studied and discussed in relation to companies). In Polish law equal treatment by public authorities is guaranteed in the Constitution (Art.32). Similarly to belief neutrality: in spite of the fact that in the public discourse breaching the rule of neutrality (mainly the religious one) is mentioned, there is a lack of systematic studies regarding the scale of this phenomenon among the public administration officials.

---

52 It is worth noticing that this rule concerns only political, not philosophical, neutrality. The only reference to the matters of philosophy regards refraining from demonstrating "close ties with individuals who are commonly known for their activity, especially political, economic, social or religious, as well as refraining from promoting any interest groups", which is related to the implementation of the principle of impartiality.

53 Prime Minister's directive on guidelines for compliance with the rules of the civil service and on the code of ethics of the civil service in 2011. – http://dokumenty.rcl.gov.pl/M2011093095301.pdf.

The principle of administration rationality is important with regards to the proper functionality of administration. The principle is included in the Civil Service Code of Ethics and it refers to the effective use of public resources to fulfill the objectives as well as the readiness of officials to prove their care for public resources and assets.

In Poland administrative decisions used to be made by persons acting on the basis of non-uniform regulations, which resulted in their different legal statuses. This situation was supposed to change with the bill on the liability of civil servants for grave infringements (*Ustawa o odpowiedzialności majątkowej funkcjonariuszy za rażące naruszenie prawa*) from 17 May 2011, whose aim was to unify mechanisms for studying the effectiveness of work done by public administration officials and conduct control, supervision, and draw appropriate conclusions regarding the staff. One of the novelties introduced by the bill is the liability of civil servants for incorrect administrative decisions. Even though the bill entered into force over two years ago, we were unable to find information concerning identified cases in which any financial penalty was imposed on civil servants.

An example of a lack of rationality in the functioning of administration might be its excessive proliferation and changes in employment structure. According to the data of the Central Statistical Office of Poland (GUS), 182,166 people were employed in administration in 2011. When we compare this data with the 2008 the number of employees rose by 19,285 persons (10.64%), and out of them 16,640 persons had permanent contracts. At the same time numerous people were employed with private-law contracts (between 2008 and 2012 their number rose by 36.85%; (Chludziński 2012). Private-law contracts were supposed to facilitate the employment of experts and specialists for special tasks, going beyond the powers of permanent employees as well as to reduce spending, and prevent criticism for increasing the number of full time positions. Their application is however contrary to the principle of full-time work for civil servants.

Increasing employment is followed by an increase in general administrative expenditure: between 2008 and 2012 the change cost PLN 10.6 billion (10.07%). These are expenses connected with new work positions: salaries and the costs of induction, training, and equipment for new employees.

Fig./Tab. 5.4: Cost of tax administration in Europe

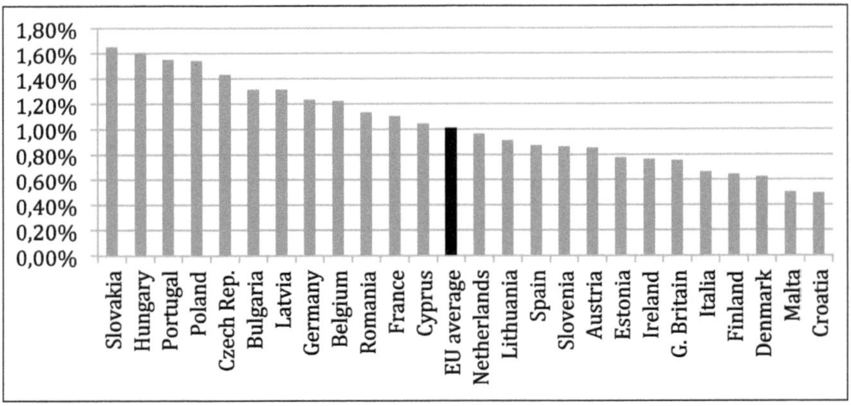

Source: www.iota-tax.org

Polish tax administration is one of the most expensive in Europe. Every year for tax collection we allocate on average 1.56% of the collected taxes[54] (Jagliński 2012). This is one of the highest indicators in Europe[55].

5.4 Effectiveness of administration (the level of executing tasks by the administration)

The effectiveness of administration is, alongside the development of an economy and democratization, a pillar of good governance. There are many definitions of good governance but every one of them underlines the meaning of the "administrative potential of governments to effectively execute the policies and public services" (*state capacity* – Good Governance Concept 2008, p. 6). Apart from the widely understood state capacity to perform its fundamental functions, there is the principle of proportionality and subsidiarity. The first one concerns the optimal and cost-effective execution of state objectives (tools for providing services and public policies

54 Average from 2008–2012.

55 Data from the Intra-European Organization of Tax Administrations (www.iota-tax.org). Data for Italy and Spain from 2011, no data for Greece and Luxembourg.

must be proportional to the objectives), the other one concerns the role of higher levels of administration towards lower levels[56].

Fig./Tab. 5.5: Selected indicators from Worldwide Governance Indicators *for Poland*

	2000	2002	2003	2004	2005	2006	2007	2008	2009	2010	2011	2012
Effectiveness of governments	0.60	0.49	0.55	0.49	0.48	0.42	0.40	0.48	0.52	0.64	0.62	0.66
Regulatory quality	0.73	0.75	0.72	0.81	0.81	0.71	0.77	0.82	0.95	0.99	0.94	0.96

Source: http://info.worldbank.org/

The effectiveness of administration is a vital element of the *Worldwide Governance Indicators* prepared by the World Bank. This report contains the indicator of effectiveness of governments (regarding their administrative potential to effectively execute the policies and public services «*state capacity*») as well as the indicator[57] of regulatory quality, which concerns formulating and implementing the regulations, mainly related to the development of the private sector.

The results (presented in table 5.5) show relatively weak results for government effectiveness even though a growing trend is clearly visible. Comparing Poland to other groups of countries demonstrates that in the last three years the assessment of Poland has been below the average for high-income OECD countries.

DAP experts believe that the national administration, despite some imperfections, functions quite effectively. An assessment of 5.20 is placed on the right side of the scale indicating a narrow margin of approval. The experts agree here that the standard deviation is small. While comparing it to the period from 5-6 years back we might notice an improvement in the effectiveness and performance of the administrative apparatus.

56 *White Paper on Good Governance*, European Commission, July 25th 2001.
57 Indicators have values from –2.5 to 2.5. A higher value means a higher level of indicator implementation.

The performance of local authorities receives an assessment similar to that of the national administration. Obviously, in the case of local authorities, unlike the administrative apparatus, the opinions consist of an average assessment of various – and often very differently functioning – institutions. Local authorities usually act fairly effectively; their assessment exceeds the medium point of the scale. Similar to the case of the national authorities, they note an improvement in effectiveness in comparison with the recent past.

Poland lacks synthetic indicators that would allow for an assessment of the administrative effectiveness at the country level; we did not manage to obtain systematic data on this matter[58]. For this reason a more detailed assessment of the effectiveness of administration, specified in relation to its specific fields of action[59] mentioned in literature, is based mainly on the quality criteria.

One of the functions of administration is **the order and regulatory function,** connected with the preservation of public law and order as well as safety. An assessment of the state of the national security system presented in the White Paper of National Security (2013, p. 9-11) is not univocally positive.

An assessment of **the servicing function**, connected with public services at the country level is extremely difficult since this issue is not studied at this level. Although there are numerous studies of the effectiveness of public services at the local level, they are non-systematic actions, which are limited by space and topic. In the audit the level of pursuing the service function in Poland will be discussed when discussing the example of education and health services.

The assessment of the condition of education in Poland is rather positive. In the OECD ranking (*Better Life Index*) Poland occupies the 7th position and becomes the leader in the region. Despite the fact that education

58 Although there are singular studies on e.g. the effectiveness of public expenditure, they were not used in the article since they covered a much earlier period than this audit. Also the Development Monitoring System supporting the process of monitoring the development and evaluation of the effects of undertaken actions for strengthening social cohesion, even though it provides us with a lot of information on the functionality of administration, it does not seem to suit our objectives.

59 Administration functions as in: *Budget Lexicon*– http://www.sejm.gov.pl/

expenditure in Poland[60] is significantly lower than the average expenditure in the European Union[61], Polish students achieve very good results at schools. It might be confirmed by a very high result in the PISA test in 2012 (Poland obtained 518 points taking the 14th position in the ranking; the average for the OECD is 497; a higher result in the region was obtained only by Estonia).

Threats and irregularities in the education system indicated by the NIK (2012a) concern first of all a decrease in the level of education in public schools, which results from faulty pedagogical supervision conducted by chief education officers and headmasters of public schools, irregularities in organizing and financing education and retraining courses for teachers as well as the functionality of special schools.

Low indicators for preschool education cannot be overlooked either. In 2011 only 69.2% of children aged 3-5 were included in the preschool education system. This indicator has gone up significantly (in 2005 it was 41%; however it remains significantly lower than the European average, which is 92.4%, as data from Eurostat show).

The Polish health service is assessed much worse. The ranking *Better Life Index*, which was quoted above, gave Poland the 27th position (out of 36) among OECD countries (countries such as Hungary and Estonia, among others, are behind Poland). One of the indicators of the effectiveness of the health service is life expectancy. On the basis of this indicator the condition of the Polish health service might be assessed relatively well (according to the OECD, life expectancy in Poland is 76.9 years; the average for OECD countries is 80 years; according to Eurostat data from 2012, the average for women in Poland is 81.1 years while it is 83.1 in the EU and respectively 77.5 and 72.7 for men). However, according to public opinion, the most serious problems that the health service struggles with is the quality of facilities providing medical treatment and the service ability in health centres (47% of the negative opinions), insufficient use of modern

60 Annual expenditure per student on primary, secondary, and university education. From: *Society at Glance* (2014).

61 Average expenditure on education in 2010 in the UE was 5.44% of GDP, in Poland it was 5.17% (the third position in the region behind Estonia and Lithuania). In 2011 this indicator fell to 4.94% (data from: Eurostat).

solutions (the Internet, electronic health insurance cards), in administration (51% of the negative opinions) and the availability of specialist physicians' medical advice and diagnostic tests (waiting time), location of centres providing these services, convenient appointment times (70% of the negative opinions – Hipsz 2012). Objective data points to a significantly higher than in EU average percentage of people who did not received necessary treatment: in Poland this indicator is 3.5% (Poland occupies the 22nd position), while the EU average is 2.2% (declarative data from Eurostat 2012).

Numerous irregularities in the functioning of the health service were also indicated in a NIK inspection. They concern predominantly unequal access for the insured to medical services, errors in contracting medical treatment and hospital indebtedness (NIK 2012a).

However, it is worth noticing that there are also strong points for the Polish health service system. The most often mentioned ones are the availability of service from general medical practitioners (73% of the positive opinions), modern medical apparatus (55% of the positive opinions) and quality of treatment (doctors' qualifications, their engagement in performed work and general approach to patients – 54% of the positive opinions). Medical assistance in emergencies is also well assessed (52% of the positive opinions) as well as the fact that there were no additional costs exceeding health insurance contributions in the National Health Fund (NFZ) (50% of the positive feedback – Hipsz 2012).

Public administration fulfils relatively well the function of **the regulator of economic development**. Regulations, which stimulate development of the private sector, seem vital from the point of view of economic development. According to the *Doing Business* report from 2014, in recent years there has been an assessment of the ease of doing business in Poland (in the general ranking, Poland occupies the 45th position out of 189; moving up 3 positions). It was influenced by significant improvement in terms of the ease of obtaining a construction permit (moving up from the 104th to the 88th position), ease of establishing a business (moving up from the 124th to the 116th position) and registering property (moving up from the 63rd to the 54th position). The key negative change concerns the ease of paying taxes (a fall from the 104th to the 113th position).

Although Poland looks quite good relative to other countries from the region in the general ranking (it is preceded only by Estonia – the 22nd position, Lithuania – the 17th position and Latvia – the 24th position), we need to note that the recorded improvement concerns first of all the areas in which Poland previously performed extremely poorly.

Among the accusations directed at regulations hindering running a business in Poland, the experts also enumerate the high risk of running a business related to frequent changes in the law, high costs of employment and a high level of criminalization of business activities, insufficient infrastructure and ineffective administration.

A NIK inspection revealed irregularities in the execution of tasks related to **the organizational function of administration** (where administrative bodies undertake constructive, independent, and creative activities, e.g. when municipal officials are trying to acquire EU funds) especially at the local level (NIK 2012a). The accusations concern an insufficient acquisition of EU funds by small units of the local authorities. The reason for this situation is first of all incorrect preparation of applications for funding (formal errors were found in 14.2% of the applications for funding which were rejected).

Another function is **the controlling and supervising function** where the state controls and supervises citizens. The sector of NGOs, which is the focus of interest of this function, is a young and still developing sphere of social life in Poland, both in terms of the law, institutions, and infrastructure. During the last dozen or so years the documents have been created which regulate and describe the way it functions, namely: legal acts, analyses, reports.

The rules for controlling citizens (voluntary work, non-profit organizations) are described in the bill on non-profit activity and on voluntary work (*Ustawa o działalności pożytku publicznego i o wolontariacie*). Since 2010 it has been obligatory to exercise control over the execution of the aforementioned bill and submit reports to the Sejm and Senate every two years. It is worth noticing that the Non-profit Activity Department (*Departament Pożytku*), in collaboration with the government and local government administration, has been preparing similar reports since 2005.

5.5 Quality of public office services

The quality of public service is best reflected in opinions of citizens themselves. According to a CBOS study, 42% of Poles (Boguszewski 2012) believe that the functioning of public offices in recent years has remained the same. 33% believe that their performance has improved (31% believe that it has rather improved, only 2% stated that it has definitely improved). 16% of the respondents noticed a worsening of the running of public offices (out of them 3% believe it has definitely deteriorated).

If we take into consideration the aspects in which the performance of public offices has improved the highest percentage of the respondents enumerate those changes which have taken place in public offices; according to 34% of Poles public officers are nicer, more friendly, more polite and tend to be smiling; 15% believe that they engage more in solving clients' problems; the same percentage appreciate the more effective and more comprehensive service provided by officials. Shortening and simplifying procedures, shorter waiting times for handling the matter at hand are also mentioned relatively often (17%) as well as better access to public offices and officials, shorter queues.

Negative changes, which are most often mentioned, include bureaucratic sprawl, complex procedures, excessively long time frames for handling matters (26%), a lack of kindness, impolite service, disregarding clients, objectification of clients (12%), and queues (11%).

5.6 Summary

Assessing the performance of public administration in Poland is not easy. Both the NIK and the DAP experts are relatively positive in their assessment of particular state functions. However, conducted inspections showed there are also numerous shortcomings in many areas. Moreover, the society also has some objections to the functioning of administration.

Polish administration is, without a doubt, extensive and costly, and, at the same time, it is not characterized by high effectiveness. Execution of the service function, related to public services and the regulation of economic development is assessed worst. Inspections connected with the protection of law and public order and state security also revealed numerous breaches. Some shortcomings were also indicated in the sphere related to tax collection.

Despite professional official staff, the rationality of the administrative structure might raise objections. Even though detailed legal regulations and codes of ethics are in place, official posts are still at risk for politicization, officials are not professional enough and practically are not held responsible for the decisions made. Complicated procedures and long time frames for handling matters were also assessed negatively.

Because of numerous recorded breaches, the general assessment of public administration is not univocally positive. Although many indicators have improved in recent years, according to Poles, official reality has not changed much.

Bibliography

Biała Księga Bezpieczeństwa Narodowego [White Paper of National Security] 2013. Available online on: http://www.spbn.gov.pl/sbn/biala-ksiega/4630,Biala-Ksiega.html (accessed on 04.18.2014).

R. Boguszewski, *Urzędowa rzeczywistość w ocenach Polaków* [Official Reality in Assessment of Poles], CBOS Report 2012. Available online on: http://www.cbos.pl/SPISKOM.POL/2012/K_146_12.PDF (accessed on 09.30.2013).

Sprawozdanie z działalności Centralnego Biura Śledczego KGP za 2012 rok [A Report on Central Bureau of Investigation of Police Headquarters in 2012], Police Headquarters, Warsaw 2012.

M. Chludziński, *Zatrudnienie w administracji rządowej – dynamika i koszty* [Employment in Government Administration – Dynamics and Costs], the Republican Foundation, Warsaw 2012. Available online on: http://republikanie.org/wp-content/uploads/2012/12/Zatrudnienie-w-administracji-rz%C4%85dowej-dynamika-i-koszty.pdf, (accessed on 02.11.2014).

A. Filak, K. Mroczka, *Ewolucja systemu służby przygotowawczej w służbie cywilnej* [Evolution of Preparatory Service System in Civil Service], in: *Administracja rządowa XXI wieku. Szanse, wyzwania i zagrożenia* [Government Administration in the 21st century. Possibilities, Challenges, and Threats], edited by J. Itrich-Drabarek, A. Filak, K. Mroczka, Warsaw 2013.

Praca nierejestrowana w Polsce 2010 r. [Unregistered Work in Poland 2010], GUS 2010. Available online on: http://www.stat.gov.pl/cps/rde/xbcr/gus/pw_praca_nierejestrowana_w_2010.pdf (accessed on 11.17.2013).

P. Heywood, J.-H. Meyer-Sahling, *Występowanie stref korupcji w zarządzaniu polską administracją rządową* [Occurrence of Corruption

Spheres in Managing Polish Government Administration], Ernst& Young, Warsaw 2008. Available online on: http://webapp01.ey.com.pl/EYP/WEB/eycom_download.nsf/resources/Korupcja_w_administracji_rzadowej.pdf/$FILE/Korupcja_w_administracji_rzadowej.pdf (accessed on 11.09.2013).

N. Hipsz, *Opinie o funkcjonowaniu systemu opieki zdrowotnej* [Opinions on Functionality of the Health Care System], CBOS Report 2012. Available online on: http://cbos.pl/SPISKOM.POL/2012/K_034_12.PDF (accessed on 04.28.2014).

K. Iszkowski, *Jak wykorzystać potencjał małych i średnich firm?* [How to Use the Potential of Small and Medium-sized Companies?], Warsaw 2012.

K. Jagliński, *Koszty i efektywność systemu podatkowego w Polsce* [Costs and Effectiveness of the Polish Tax System], Republican Foundation, Warsaw 2013. Available online on: http://cafr.pl/raport-koszty-i-efektywnosc-systemu-podatkowego-w-polsce/ (accessed on 12.10.2013).

K. Łuba, *Transparentność postępowania administracyjnego poprzez wprowadzenie metryki do Kodeksu postępowania administracyjnego* [Transparency of Administrative Proceedings by Introduction of Case Sheet into the Code of Administrative Proceedings], in: *Administracja rządowa XXI wieku. Szanse, wyzwania i zagrożenia* [Government Administration in the 21st century. Potential, Challenges, and Threats], edited by J. Itrich-Drabarek, A. Filak, K. Mroczka, Warsaw 2013.

Post-inspection Speech 2008, NIK 2008. Available online on: http://www.mf.gov.pl/c/document_library/get_file?uuid=751adae2-b177-4d00-b748-4175e90bbcd8&groupId=764034 (accessed on 02.02. 2014).

Informacja o wynikach kontroli poboru podatku dochodowego od osób fizycznych 2010 [Information on findings in the inspection of personal income tax collection 2010], NIK 2010. Available online on: http://www.nik.gov.pl/plik/id,1594,vp,1781.pdf (accessed on 02.02. 2014).

A Report on the NIK for 2012. Available online on: http://www.nik.gov.pl/plik/id,5017.pdf (accessed on 02.02. 2014).

Audyt wewnętrzny w systemie kontroli zarządczej 2012 [Internal Audit in Management Control System 2012]. Available online on: http://www.

nik.gov.pl/kontrole/wyniki-kontroli-nik/pobierz,nik-P-11-022-audyt.pdf,typ,kk.pdf (accessed on 01.16.2014).

E. Nowacka, *Polski samorząd terytorialny* [Polish Local Government], Warsaw 2006.

Analysis of Economic Situation in Poland (OECD Economic Survey POLAND). Available online on: http://www.oecd.org/eco/49971872.pdf (accessed on 01.18.2014).

Raport o stanie edukacji 2012 [A Report on Education 2012]. Available online on: http://eduentuzjasci.pl/publikacje-ee-lista/raporty/150-raport-o-stanie-edukacji/816-raport-o-stanie-edukacji-2012-licza-sie-efekty.html (accessed on 04.20.2014).

Z. Rau, *Wyniki badań świadków koronnych – empiryczne badania porównawcze w latach 2001, 2009 i 2012* [Findings on Key Witnesses – empirical comparative studies in 2001, 2009 and 2012], "Prawo I Prokuratura" 2013, No. 5.

F. Schneider, *Size and Development of the Shadow Economies of Portugal and 35 other OECD Countries from 2003 to 2013: Some New Facts*, 2013. Available online on: http://www.econ.jku.at/members/Schneider/files/publications/2013/ShadEcEurope31_Jan2013.pdf (accessed on 01.20.2014).

Society at a glance 2014: OECD social indicators. Available online on:http://www.oecd-ilibrary.org/social-issues-migration-health/society-at-a-glance-2014_soc_glance-2014-en (accessed on 04.24.2014).

Z. Wojciechowski, *Dualistyczny model administracji na szczeblu wojewódzkim w Polsce. Próba oceny* [Dualistic Model of Administration At the Voivodeship Level in Poland. An Attempt of Evaluation], in: *Administracja rządowa XXI wieku* [Government Administration in the 21st century], as cited.

Prime Minister's directive on guidelines for compliance with the rules of the civil service and on the code of ethics of the civil service in 2011. Available online on: http://dokumenty.rcl.gov.pl/M2011093095301.pdf (accessed on 04.04.2014).

6. Democracy in the society

An assessment of the Polish democracy would not be complete without understanding what this system means for citizens. Various definitions of democracy highlight the importance of different principles for recognizing a given system as democratic. The results discussed below make it possible to tell whether formal definition of democracy corresponds to what citizens believe is important for a democratic state. Conducted analyses also allow for an assessment of the performance of democracy and its selected principles in Poland.

Survey data, although seemingly the best way to learn about public opinion, is an imperfect source since it does not fully reflect the actual picture of the world. However, it constitutes a reliable source of information on some trends.

6.1 Understanding democracy

6.1.1 Social definition of democracy

Democracy is often defined minimally as a system in which individuals in power are chosen in free elections (Schumpeter 1942, Przeworski 1999). Participation in elections is a type of political activity which ensures equal access to politics for all citizens and, at the same time, it assures the engagement of a relatively large number of citizens in all world democracies. It is no surprise then that free and equal elections were judged to be the key feature of democracy. The meaning of elections is underlined by other features too. They are believed to be critical for judging a state as democratic: universal suffrage (average 3.82), selection of the most valuable individuals to rule (average 3.82), and the possibility of punishing a bad government by removing it from power (average 3.8). Free elections are key for all these phenomena to occur.

Fig./Tab. 6.1: Democratic standards in Poland – average values of significance and the level of implementation of democratic features

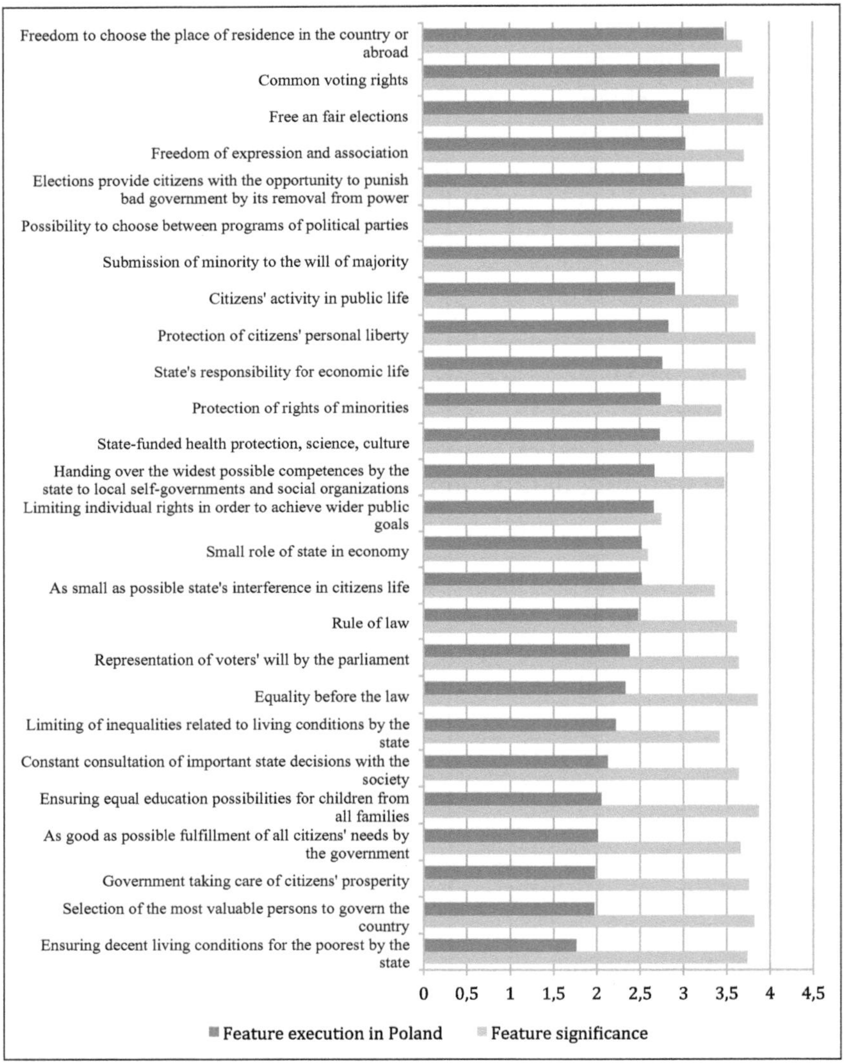

Source: CBOS/DAP – Feliksiak 2013

According to respondents, state redistributive functions are also significant from the point of view of a democratic state. The second position, following free and honest elections, is, in the respondents' opinion, ensuring equal education opportunities for children from all families (average 3.87). Further on the list are: state-funded health protection, education, and culture (average 3.82), government taking care of citizens' prosperity (average 3.76), the state ensuring that the poorest have decent living conditions (average 3.74).

The results of conducted studies show that an ideal democracy in Poland is far from having been achieved. The majority of the democratic features are not present at a satisfactory level. Only in the case of two principles (freedom to choose one's place of residence either in the country or abroad, as well as universal suffrage) do most respondents strongly agree with the statement that they are observed in Poland. The operation of the welfare state (the state ensuring that the poorest have decent living conditions, the government taking care of citizens' prosperity, ensuring equal education opportunities for children from all types of families) is assessed badly. Negative opinions prevail in assessment of authority-citizen relations (selection of the most qualified individuals to rule the country, the best possible meeting of all citizens' needs by the government, the authorities' taking into account the opinions of the citizens).

Are the characteristics of an ideal democracy universal? An analysis of the data from the European Social Survey (Fig. 6.2) shows that when it comes to thinking of an ideal democracy, Poles are clearly not that different from inhabitants of mature democracies and post-communist democracies. Four features of democracy which were judged by Poles to be the most significant do not differ from those enumerated by inhabitants of the other European countries (even though they are enumerated in a different order). The situation is similar in terms of features judged the least important.

Fig./Tab. 6.2: In your opinion, for a democracy, how important is it generally

	Poland		Mature democracies		Post-communist democracies	
	Average	Std.	Average	Std.	Average	Std.
that courts treat all citizens equally?	9.60	1.14	9.33	1.42	8.85	1.91
that the media provide citizens with reliable information that allows for an assessment of the government?	9.35	1.36	8.76	1.81	8.73	1.84
that the government explains its decisions to the voters?	9.32	1.28	8.94	1.56	8.74	1.80
that constitutional courts have the ability to hold the government back from acting when it exceeds its powers?	9.29	1.44	8.92	1.71	8.78	1.87
that parliamentary elections are free and honest?	9.27	1.44	9.01	1.60	8.85	1.77
that the government protects all citizens from poverty?	9.05	1.79	8.64	1.88	8.57	2.05
that parties which ruled badly are punished by voters with a worse result than in previous elections?	8.92	1.65	8.44	1.93	8.49	2.03
that citizens have an authoritative voice in the key political issues by deciding directly in a referendum?	8.83	1.75	8.14	2.06	8.46	1.97

that rights of various minority groups are protected?	8.80	1.77	8.58	1.83	8.16	2.20
that the government undertakes actions to decrease differences in income?	8.70	2.08	7.93	2.24	8.24	2.31
that migrants gain the right to participate in parliamentary elections only after they have obtained citizenship of the state they decided to reside in?	8.49	2.09	8.03	2.39	7.96	2.44
that the media have the ability to criticize the government?	8.42	2.24	8.16	2.15	8.46	2.00
that opposition parties have the ability to criticize the government?	8.39	2.07	8.33	2.01	8.36	2.03
that particular political parties are a real alternative for each other and clearly differ from each other?	8.17	2.08	7.68	2.11	8.39	2.01
that voters, before they decide who they want to vote for, discuss political issues with their family and friends?	7.76	2.56	7.35	2.39	7.56	2.54
that politicians, before making decisions, take into account the opinion of governments of other European countries?	6.35	2.70	6.80	2.43	6.63	2.52

Source: ESS – own calculations

In the perception of Poles, their country performs similarly across a range of features with other democracies (Fig.6.3). It is, however, worth noticing that the high expectations of Poles in relation to their concept of an ideal democracy lead to a much higher disparity than in other countries between their ideal and the democracy's actual functioning.

Fig./Tab. 6.3: In your country

	Poland		Mature democracies		Post-communist democracies	
	Average	Std.	Average	Std	Average	Std
Do the media have the ability to criticize the government?	7.75	2.41	7.88	2.20	6.89	2.62
Do opposition parties, i.e. those not part of the government, have the ability to criticize it?	7.60	2.39	7.99	2.06	6.92	2.61
Are the Sejm elections free and honest?	7.37	2.64	8.10	2.22	6.05	2.97
Do voters, before deciding who to vote for, discuss political issues with their family and friends?	6.50	2.59	6.44	2.30	6.54	2.62
Are particular political parties a real alternative for each other; do they clearly differ from each other?	6.23	2.59	5.84	2.37	5.55	2.68
Are the rights of various minority groups protected?	6.14	2.30	6.49	2.42	6.45	2.82

Do the media provide citizens with reliable information allowing for an assessment of the government?	5.90	2.61	6.28	2.46	5.73	2.60
Are parties which ruled badly punished by voters with a worse result than in the previous elections?	5.61	2.93	6.11	2.82	4.67	3.25
Do politicians, before making decisions, take into account the opinions of governments of other European countries?	5.35	2.33	5.76	2.26	5.17	2.59
Do citizens have an authoritative voice in the key political issues by deciding about them directly in a referendum?	4.94	2.93	4.73	3.22	4.47	3.01
Do courts treat all people equally?	3.90	2.66	5.82	3.08	3.66	2.83
Does the government explain its decisions to the voters?	3.64	2.46	4.95	2.70	3.56	2.76
Does the government protect all citizens from poverty?	3.00	2.42	4.73	2.84	2.93	2.73
Does the government undertake actions for lowering differences in income?	2.99	2.41	4.49	2.62	2.83	2.65

Source: ESS – own calculations

6.2 Legitimization of the political system

6.2.1 Acceptance of the political system

The level of satisfaction with the execution of particular principles of democracy, especially those judged by citizens as the key ones from the point of view of a democratic state, is correlated with support for this system. From the perspective of the stability of the democratic system, diffuse support (for democracy as being the best system) is key.

Studies conducted by CBOS confirm that Poles consider democracy as the only game in town (Feliksiak 2013). Similar results are seen in an analysis of conditional support for democracy.

Fig./Tab. 6.4: Support for democracy

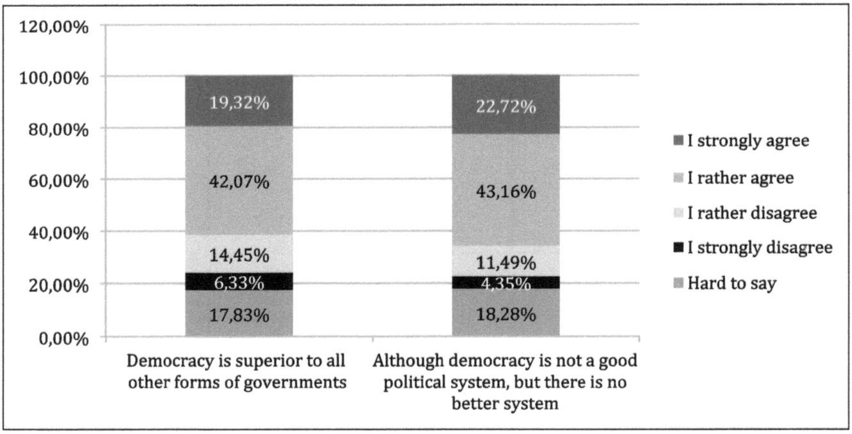

Source: CBOS/DAP – Feliksiak 2013

Support for democracy shows significant stability over time (Fig.6.5). From 2001 to 2013 there were insignificant fluctuations both in the percentage of individuals who agree and disagree with the analyzed statement (only after the elections in 2007 do we notice a dramatic growth in the number of people believing that democracy prevails over all the other types of governance; however, after a few months the level returned to the state from before November 2007). It means that, regardless of the assessment of the effectiveness of functioning of current authorities and institutions, citizens regard democracy not only as the only possible political system, but also as the best.

Fig./Tab. 6.5: Opinions on democracy

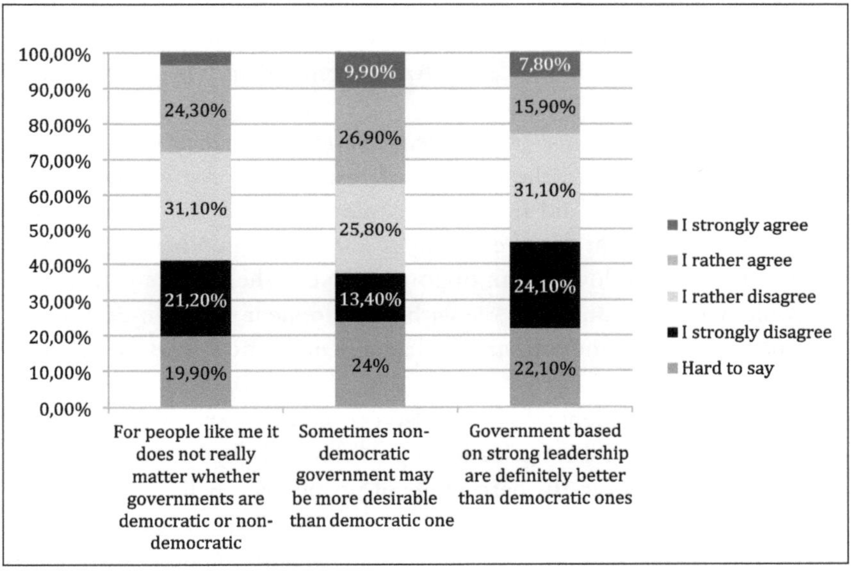

Source: CBOS/DAP – Feliksiak 2013

Due to the considerable support for democracy as the best system, it might be surprising that one-third of the respondents believe that it does not matter whether there is democratic or non-democratic governance (13% strongly agree, 24% rather agree-Fig.6.6), while only every fifth Pole strongly disagrees with this statement. The level of political alienation measured in this way changes over time. From 2000 to 2006 the percentage of people for whom the governance system did not matter ranged between 40% and 50%. This ratio changed drastically during the election campaign in 2007 when the number of respondents convinced that governance type does not matter drastically decreased. Since that time, the number of citizens who identify with democracy has prevailed over the number of alienated ones.

Support for democracy does not preclude acceptance of non-democratic governance: 36.8% of respondents (both from the group convinced that democracy prevails over all the other forms of governance, and from among the respondents who disagree with this statement) believe that sometimes non-democratic governance might be more desirable than democratic. Almost a half of respondents disagree with this statement. It is also important to note that every fourth respondent has no opinion on the matter.

The level of acceptance of non-democratic governance was changing similarly to the trend in the number of respondents for whom a given state's political system did not matter; mid-2007 was the turning point and since then, except for the spring of 2010, the number of potential supporters has been lower than opponents. Nevertheless, the percentages of people who agree and disagree with the statement that non-democratic governance might be more desirable than a democratic system, are at similar levels.

Among the respondents there are also people who express the view that governance based on strong leadership is definitely better than a democratic system. However, the percentage of people who believe in the superiority of an authoritarian regime (24.7%) is significantly lower than the percentage of respondents who disapprove of non-democratic solutions (54.4%). These values are relatively stable over time.

6.2.2 Assessment of the performance of democracy

An important element of support for democracy, apart from general acceptance of the system, is the specific support expressed by satisfaction with actions undertaken by specific authorities in a given place and at a given time. These two types of support might be independent of each other, which is the case in Poland: although the majority of Poles are convinced of the superiority of democracy over other types of governance, only one-third (34.9%) are currently satisfied with its functionality in Poland (2% are highly satisfied, 32.9% are rather satisfied). As many as 16.9% of respondents declare a high level of dissatisfaction with the functionality of this system, while 40.6% are rather dissatisfied.

Fig./Tab. 6.6: Assessment of the performance of democracy

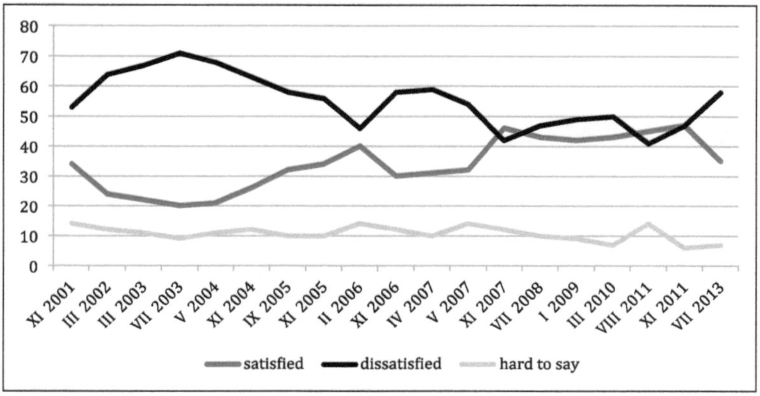

Source: CBOS

The percentage of Poles satisfied and dissatisfied with the performance of democracy changes over time (Fig.6.6). From 2001 to 2007 the percentage of those dissatisfied significantly exceeded the number of those satisfied with the functionality of democracy; but it was following a downward trend. Even though from 2007 to 2011 the percentages of those satisfied and those dissatisfied remained at a similar level, and during the election period in 2007 and again in 2011 there was even a short-term majority of those satisfied with the performance of democracy, since the end of 2011 there has been a significant growth of dissatisfaction with the functionality of the system.

According to the data in the European Social Survey, an average level of performance of democracy in Poland is slightly higher than in other post-communist democracies (the average values[62] are respectively 4.91 and 4.40), and at the same time lower than in mature democracies in Western Europe (5.67).

6.2.3 Confidence in democratic institutions

A CBOS study asked questions about confidence in selected public institutions. The results show that the level of confidence in democratic

62 Average values based on responses regarding satisfaction with democracy displayed on a scale of 11 points where 0 means extreme dissatisfaction and 10 extreme satisfaction. The standard deviation is given in brackets.

institutions in Poland is relatively low (Tab.6.8). In 2012 half of Poles did not trust the government, 55% distrusted the Parliament, while 65% did not trust political parties (Cybulska 2012[63]). These results change over time.

Fig./Tab. 6.7: Do you generally trust or not the listed institutions?

	2002		2004		2006		2008		2010		2012	
	Yes	No	Yes	No	Yes	No	Yes	No	Yes	No	Yes	No
Government	42%	45%	21%	68%	47%	40%	56%	32%	31%	60%	39%	49%
Sejm and Senate	28%	54%	21%	67%	30%	54%	39%	44%	21%	68%	29%	55%
Political parties	15%	65%	13%	72%	24%	61%	28%	54%	14%	76%	20%	65%

Source: CBOS – Cybulska 2012

The level of confidence in Parliament in Poland is among the lowest levels found in Europe (according to ESS data).

Fig./Tab. 6.8: Confidence in the Parliament

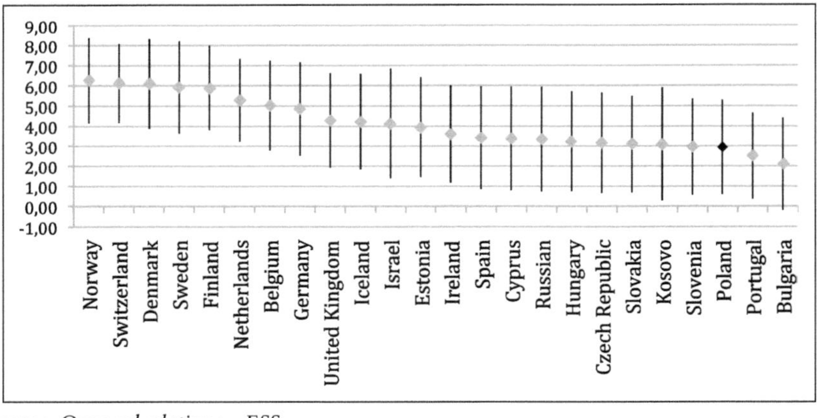

Source: Own calculations – ESS

63 A study entitled *Current Problems and Affairs* (260) was conducted from the 5th to 11th January 2012 on a representative sample of 1058 random adult inhabitants of Poland.

An average level of confidence in the Parliament places Poland on one of the lowest places among the analyzed European states. It is worth noting that the level of confidence in the Parliament in mature democracies is generally higher than in post-communist democracies.

Confidence in political parties in Poland is even lower than in parliament – barely every fifth Pole trusts them. The level of confidence in parties in the last decade has been gradually increasing. The lowest level was recorded in 2002 and 2004: parties were trusted respectively by 15% and 14% of the population. The highest amount of confidence was enjoyed by political parties in 2008, but even then only every third Pole trusted them. The only EU states, which Poland does not fall behind in terms of trust in parties and politicians, are: Spain, Portugal, and Bulgaria.

Fig./Tab. 6.9: Confidence in political parties

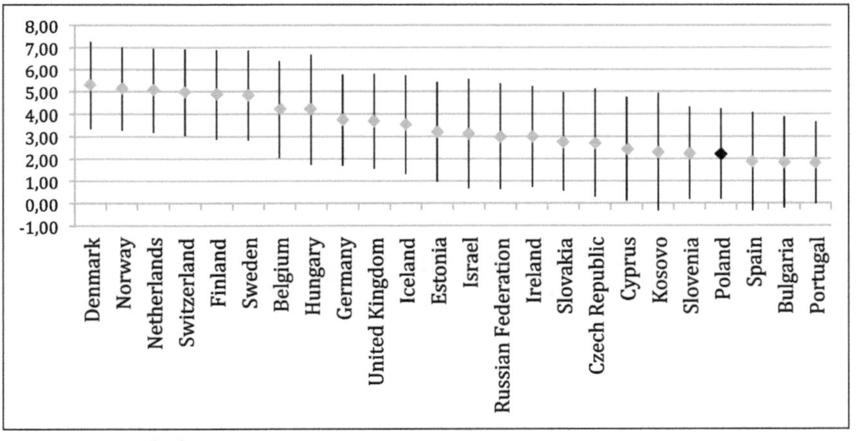

Source: Own calculations – ESS

In terms of confidence in political parties, it is Denmark, Norway, the Netherlands, and Switzerland that are characterized by the highest levels. Among the new democracies Hungary is the leader and it occupies the 7th position in the ranking.

Fig./Tab. 6.10: Confidence in politicians

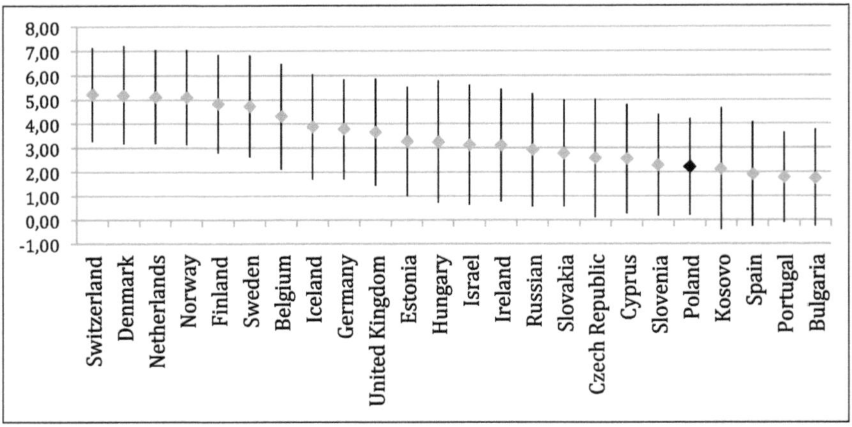

Source: Own calculations – ESS

6.3 Democracy at the local level

6.3.1 Readiness to participate in decision-making process (on the local level).

Citizen participation in politics is key for democracy. It is stressed both by theorists of the topic and citizens themselves, who perceive elections and citizen activity as one of the most important features of democracy.

The level of citizen activity in Poland is very low. The country is characterized by very low turnout, a low percentage of respondents also admit participating in other types of political activity: over a half of the questioned (54%) have never participated in any type of citizen activity (Feliksiak 2012)[64].

64 A study entitled *Current Problems and Affairs* (268) conducted from the 5th to 16th September 2012 on a representative sample of 985 random adult inhabitants of Poland.

Fig./Tab. 6.11: Has the respondent in the last twelve months

	Poland		Mature democracies		Post-communist democracies	
	Yes	No	Yes	No	Yes	No
contacted a politician, of the government or the local government level?	7.3%	92.7%	15.0%	85.0%	7.4%	92.6%
worked for political party or organization social?	2.5%	97.5%	4.5%	95.5%	2.6%	97.4%
worked for a different type of organization or association?	7.1%	92.9%	22.1%	77.9%	3.8%	96.2%
worn or placed in a visible place a badge/sticker promoting a campaign or event?	4.4%	95.6%	7.8%	92.2%	4.6%	95.4%
signed a petition?	10.4%	89.6%	31.1%	68.9%	11.4%	88.6%
participated in a legal demonstration?	2.3%	97.7%	9.6%	90.4%	4.5%	95.5%
boycotted anything-intentionally refrained from purchasing selected goods, products?	5.7%	94.3%	24.0%	76.0%	7.3%	92.7%

Source: Own calculations – ESS

The level of civil activity in Poland is significantly lower than in the mature democracies of Western Europe. The largest differences are visible in the case of activity in associations (in Western Europe every fifth respondent is active in them), signing petitions (every third inhabitant of Western Europe did that), as well as boycotting selected products and goods (every fourth citizen of mature democracies).

Comparing Poland to other post-communist democracies shows that the level of local activity in the countries of the region is similar. Poland is characterized only by a slightly lower percentage of citizens active in organizations and associations and a slightly lower percentage of citizens participating in legal demonstrations or boycotting selected products.

6.3.2 Subjective influence on the local level

The low percentage of people undertaking civil activities might result from a lack of a sense of influence and efficacy in state matters. As many as 79% of Poles believe they have no impact on matters decided by the state (40% definitely think so); only every fifth respondent is convinced of having an influence on the country matters (3% strongly; Pankowski 2013). A slightly higher percentage (42%) unveils a sense of influence on the city or municipality level; however, half of respondents (56%) believe that they have no impact on the matters of their local community.

Generally, the data show that every fourth Pole thinks that he/she only has an influence on the matters of the city or municipality; this percentage has virtually not changed during the last year. However, the percentage of respondents convinced they impact both the state and the city/municipality matters has decreased (during last year there was a fall in the percentage points).

In the long run, the sense of efficacy and influence on the country level is subject to slight fluctuations; the trend however remains intact. When it comes to the local level from 2010 to 2012 we notice a growth in the sense that one can influence the matters of the municipality/city (the percentage of affirmative responses exceeded the percentage of negative ones). Since 2012 subjective influence on local matters (and on the state too) has been systematically decreasing.

6.3.3 Confidence in local authorities

The level of confidence in local authorities (of cities/municipalities) turns out to be relatively high, when compared to the other analyzed institutions.

Tab./Fig. 6.12: Confidence in local authorities

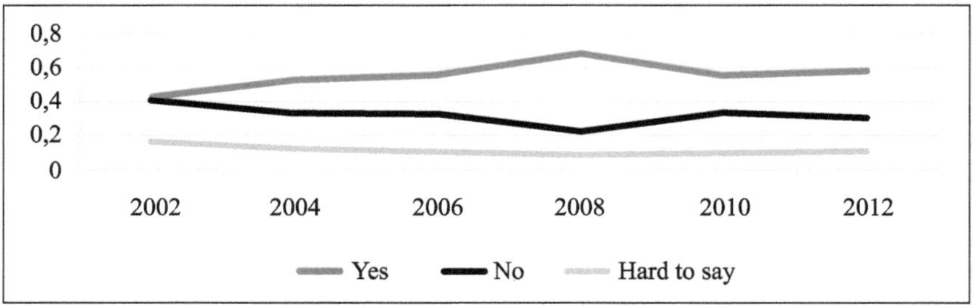

Source: CBOS – Cybulska 2012

The percentage of people who declare that they have strong or relatively strong confidence in the abovementioned authorities has been exceeding the percentage of the distrustful since 2004 (in 2002 both groups were almost identical in numbers). The highest growth of confidence was recorded in 2008. However, two years later the percentage of people in this group drastically fell to the level registered in 2004.

Tab./Fig. 6.13: To what extent does the development of your town and its closest region depend on ...

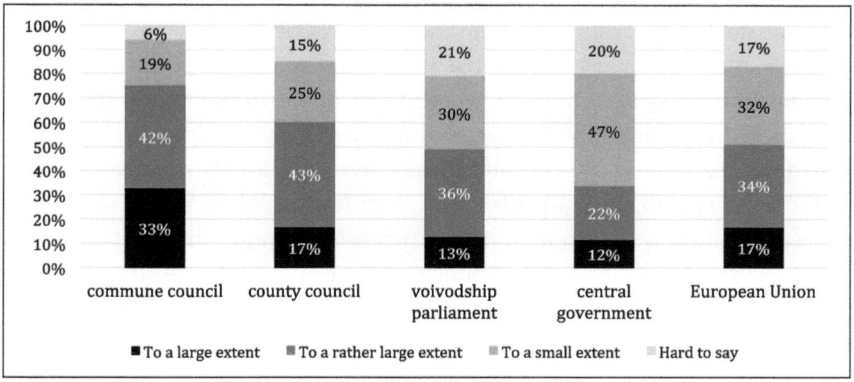

Source: CBOS/DAP – Pankowski 2013

Do local authorities take care of their region and its citizens? According to Poles[65], the development of their town and the closest region is to the greatest extent dependent upon the commune authorities (32.6%). Almost one-fifth of those questioned believe that county authorities (17%) or the European Union (17%) are responsible for the development of their area. It is the government in Warsaw that contributes least to the development of their place of living.

65 A study entitled *Current Problems and Affairs* (278) was conducted from the 4th to 11th July 2013 on a representative sample of 1005 random adult inhabitants of Poland.

6.4 Summary

There clearly exists general support for democracy in Poland. Despite relatively high level of acceptance for non-democratic solutions, the majority of Poles believe that democracy is the best system. Yet the performance of particular aspects of democracy and fulfilment of these normative expectations is far from satisfactory. In particular democratic institutions are assessed poorly

International comparative studies demonstrate that Poland does not differ a lot from other European democracies in terms of the normative ideal of democracy they embrace: the same set of features (although in a slightly different order) is believed to be vital from the point of view of the democratic system both by inhabitants of post-communist democracies, including Poland, and citizens of mature Western democracies. What distinguishes Poland are the high normative expectations concerning the implementation of the principles of democracy, especially in the social justice sphere and in the domain of politicians' accountability, which seems to be the reason for high discrepancies between the democratic ideal and its implementation. A comparison of the performance of democracy shows that inhabitants of Western Europe are more satisfied with how the system works than citizens of post-communist democracies.

In spite of a relatively high democratic awareness, the Polish democracy is influenced by low social capital: citizens have limited confidence in public institutions, and low sense of influence on state and local matters. Because of this they do not participate in politics at both, the local and the national level. The low level of social capital proves that the civil society in Poland, whose working is extremely important from the point of view of the proper functioning of democracy, proves underdeveloped.

Bibliography

A. Cybulska, *Zaufanie społeczne* [Social Confidence], CBOS Report 2012. Available online on: http://www.cbos.pl/SPISKOM.POL/2012/K_033_12.PDF (accessed on 10.03.2013).

D. Easton, *A re-assessment of the Concept of Political Support*, "British Journal of Political Science" 1975, v. 5, part 4.

M. Feliksiak, *Poczucie wpływu na sprawy publiczne i zaangażowanie obywatelskie* [Sense of Influence on Public Matters and Civil Engagement], CBOS Report 2012. Available online on: http://www.cbos.pl/SPISKOM.POL/2012/K_142_12.PDF (accessed on 11.15.2013).

M. Feliksiak, *Polacy o demokracji* [Poles On Democracy], CBOS Report 2013. Available online on: http://www.cbos.pl/SPISKOM.POL/2013/K_125_13.PDF (accessed on 10.03.2013).

K. Pankowski, *Potencjał niezadowolenia społecznego – stosunek do różnych form protestu* [Social Dissatisfaction Potential – approach to various forms of protests], CBOS Report 2013. Available online on: http://www.cbos.pl/SPISKOM.POL/2013/K_055_13.PDF (accessed on 11.13.2013).

T. Szawiel, *Kryzys demokracji a poparcie systemu politycznego w Polsce* [Democracy Crisis versus Support of Political System in Poland], in: *Populizm a demokracja* [Populism versus Democracy], edited by R. Markowski, Warsaw: ISP PAN, 2004, p. 145–171.

7. Political process

7.1 Democratic elections as an instrument for selecting power

7.1.1 An analysis of Polish electoral law

In reviewing Polish electoral law, it should be noted that it is both stable and its specific provisions resemble those existing in other democratic countries. Polish electoral law is in accordance with the constitutional requirement of "proportionality." Since August 1st, 2011, the Electoral Law has been in force. It contains regulations for national parliamentary and presidential, as well as regional and EU parliamentary elections based on the principles of universality, equality, directness, and secrecy of voting. In the majority of Polish elections these principles are respected properly and, as a consequence, and therefore the reliability of the electoral procedure is not in question. International agencies monitoring free and fair elections perceive Polish elections equally positively.

The body of Polish electoral law was crafted at the beginning of the 1990s. Parliamentary elections take place in accordance with proportional representation with "open" (the type of ballot that requires voting for a specific candidate, featuring on a particular party list) electoral lists in constituencies of a dozen or so mandates. This type of representation usually leads to the creation of a multiparty system, and as a consequence, to coalition governments. The same pattern persists in Polish polity.

From 1989 to 2008 the Senate was elected according to the majority voting system in the constituencies of two or three (from 2001 also four) mandates. Since 2011 senators have been elected in single member districts with a simple majority. It is worth stressing that a change in the electoral rules for the Senate and especially its justification is contrary to widely accepted political science knowledge on how such an electoral system works. A common belief in Poland that the new rules will result in less partisan and more socially-determined composition of the Senate has failed.

If anything in social sciences comes close to be nominated a "law," it is certainly the so-called Duverger's Law, according to which introducing a plurality system in single-member districts leads to a two-party system.

7.1.2 Autonomy of the institutions organizing elections

The National Electoral Commission (PKW) is an executive body appointed by the President of the Republic of Poland. The process of organizing elections during the whole democratic period since 1989 has been satisfactory. No international organization has raised any objections to the functioning of this institution. However, two features of the National Electoral Commission are worth critical comments. First of all, it is an extremely conservative body. Its representatives some deliberately refrain from taking part in public debate to clarify the substance and procedures of electoral democracy. Secondly, the National Electoral Commission consists exclusively of lawyers, which results in law being treated as reality. We believe that changes towards a more interdisciplinary composition of the Polish National Electoral Commission are necessary. Moreover, let us emphasize that expert opinions at our disposal point to a very high, almost maximum rating of the functioning of this institution.

7.1.3 Areas outside elected institutions' control.

From the formal and legal point of view, Polish legal regulations do not differ a great deal from European ones. Institutions designed for specific treatment are subject to complex control and supervising procedures. There are ways to assess their activities through parliamentary commissions or the Sejm as a whole. Recently, especially from 2012 to 2013, we did not experience any irregularities in the functionality of these institutions. The military and special forces in Poland are (similarly to other democracies) indirectly controlled by the elected bodies.

Fig./Tab. 7.1: Civil control over …

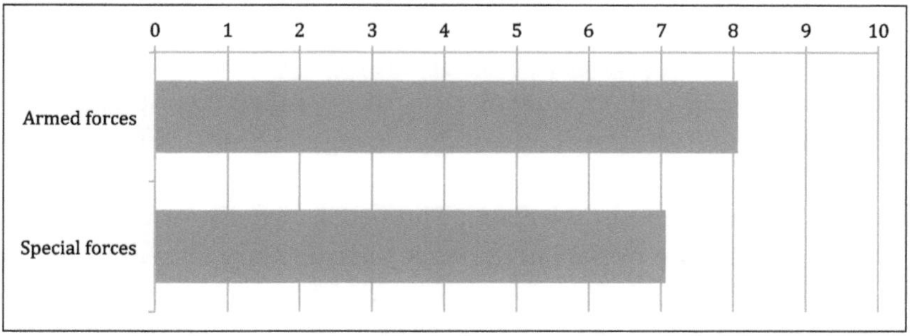

Source: DAP expert survey. Average on a scale from 0 to 10

Our experts perceive the discussed issue similarly. The civil control over the military and secret services was assessed positively and control over the armed forces raises no substantive doubts. However, with regard to the way services such as the Internal Security Agency (ABW) or the Central Anti-Corruption Bureau (CBA) operate, substantial differences of views among our experts unveil. Still, generally our experts believe that in Poland there are no important security/intelligence institutions operating outside the law, i.e. cases in which informal dismissal from one's duties or special treatment and privileged relations with the authorities are in place.

Fig./Tab. 7.2: Institutions operating outside of the law

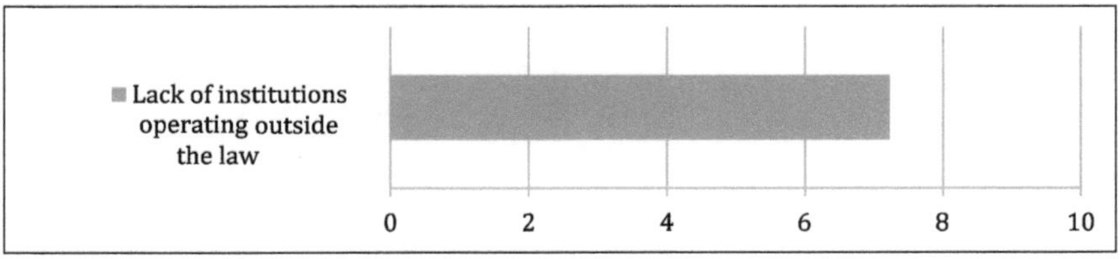

Source: DAP expert survey. Average on a scale from 0 to 10

The respondents who noticed that there are institutions using various types of formal and informal privileges pointed at the church in general and the Roman Catholic Church in particular.

7.1.4 An assessment of turnover in government

Since limiting the powers of the President of the Republic of Poland at the beginning of the 1990s regarding specifically the president's ability to dismiss parliament as well as implementing the so-called "constructive vote of no confidence," the possibility of dismissing the Prime Minister by the Sejm without appointing a successor, bringing about a change of government has become more problematic. This equals stability of the executive power. A change of government during a parliamentary term must be preceded by putting together a new governmental majority able to vote for a constructive motion of censure. So far the mechanism has not been activated. Since implementing the new Constitution, that is, since 1997, seven attempts have been undertaken to shorten the term of the Sejm and only one of them (on September 7th, 2007) succeeded. Therefore, the adopted mechanisms stabilize the Polish political system and, at the same time, allow for making a fundamental change in the political configuration if voters consider the development as diverging from democratic standards.

7.2 Voting rights

The issue of citizen voting rights is the key element in assessing democracies, especially in the case of young democracies. Most internationally significant projects assessing this aspect of Polish democracy (BTI, FH or *Rule of Law Index*) leave no room for doubt that elections in Poland are free and fair and discrimination in terms of access to voting, if it appears, is of a marginal and unintentional character and has no impact on the final election results. They also point to the fact that the Polish electoral law affords special treatment to candidates from national minorities who are exempted from clearing the 5% all-national threshold in the Sejm elections, proving its high democratic standards. A similar assessment can be found in the *Rule of Law Index* report, where such aspects of democracy as "freedom of expression and beliefs" or "freedom of assembly and association" are discussed.

7.2.1 Conditions for vote casting and barriers in voting

Despite the general positive assessment of the issues connected with the practical application of voting rights, namely the conditions of casting one's vote and barriers in access to voting, let's note that the low electoral turnout in Polish parliamentary or local elections (usually below 50% of eligible voters) calls for deeper consideration. The problem is the real scope of the so-called involuntary absence, a situation in which a voter is willing and ready to actively participate in the election, however, for various reasons, voter's intentions are not materialized. In the last parliamentary elections of 2011 for the first time Poles had the option of casting their vote through a representative or by mail (mail ballot). The former option is available, however, to two cases: to individuals suffering from "severe or moderate" disabilities and to individuals over 75 years of age. It remains unknown why for instance a serious illness or other significant circumstances cannot provide the basis for appointing a representative. Additionally, the very procedure of properly drawing up documentation for the to-be-representative seems too complex and hedged around with numerous technical conditions.

The Polish experience with the mail ballot in 2011 is not encouraging as well – only 22 thousand citizens (out of several million) and fewer than a thousand disabled citizens cast their vote using the new method. A public opinion poll tells us however that public knowledge on the topic of new forms of electoral participation is not only limited but also inaccurate (for instance a significant percentage of Poles believe that currently they can vote electronically).

7.2.2 Ensuring conditions for free elections

The latest parliamentary elections in 2011 did not demonstrate any serious or even less serious irregularities in terms of voting freedom. This is how it looks from the formal side and this is how it is assessed by international institutions. Our experts assess it similarly, as 11 issues related to legal regulations for the reliable conducting of parliamentary elections are assessed at the highest level and practical "freedom of choice in voting" is assessed on a level of 7.2 (the average assessment is 9.1). A survey conducted on a representative group of Poles shows that for the vast majority the essence of democracy is "free and fair elections" (72%) and freedom to express their opinions (77%).

The issue having the greatest impact on the freedom of elections or lack thereof is the role of the Catholic Church in Poland. And again there are no systematic studies of this problem. There are nonetheless some indirect ones and they conclude that even though in 1999, 69% of Poles stated that it bothered them when priests "would tell people how to vote," in 2005 this percentage increased to 80%, and in 2011 to 86% (CBOS data for the year 1999 and PGSW for the years 2005 and 2011). In the quoted study an additional question was asked, namely whether the Catholic Church has been engaged in the electoral campaign of 2011 and 34% of Poles responded positively to this question. Additionally, Poles almost unanimously (89%) pointed at the fact that the Catholic Church engaged politically by taking the side of one particular party (only 5% pointed at all the other parties).

7.2.3 Electoral law abuses

International rankings (BTI, RoL, HF) do not register any electoral fraud in Poland. Reality is a bit more complex, though since, as local elections show, the possibility of buying votes especially in regions affected by structural unemployment or poor regions constitutes a serious threat to the reliability of the results in the local context (*vide* the local elections in Walbrzych in 2010 and their invalidation).

The problem is that the electoral code does not make it possible for national observers to be present in polling stations, although it allows foreign observers to be present. NGOs dealing with this matter want to change this bizarre provision.

In an interesting and detailed study (Wąsik 2012) several conclusions are worth quoting here, namely: (a) Electoral fraud is a marginal phenomenon; (b) The recorded irregularities do not pose a threat for the democratic order in Poland; (c) The harmfulness of electoral irregularities mainly means that they are highly publicized, which leads to discouragement and increased levels of political cynicism and apathy with regards to the electoral democracy and politics; (d) The economic factor (poverty) is the most important driving force for committing a crime by a voter; (e) Law enforcement authorities deal relatively well with the detection of electoral criminal offences, which most often ends with finding the accused guilty. However, there is a problem with a significant percentage of preparatory proceedings being discharged.

With regards to the aforementioned irregularities and abuses of polling streams, consideration should be given to the replacement of representatives of polling streams with individuals belonging to the civil service who will be trained in terms of substance. It also seems necessary to consider manifestly unfounded the prohibition of letting national observers onto the grounds of polling streams.

7.3 Running for Office

7.3.1 Running for office: legal mechanisms

In terms of the issue of the right to vote and the right to stand in elections Polish law is quite liberal, especially when it comes to the age of the candidate (a senator should be above 30 years of age and a candidate for the presidential office – 35). The right to vote and stand for election is endowed to every Polish citizen. Moreover, the citizens of other EU member states have the right to vote in European parliamentary elections and local elections in Poland after compliance with the domicile requirement.

Mechanisms for denying the right to vote concern precisely defined situations, especially in the following cases: deprivation of public rights by court decision, denying the right to vote by the decision of the State Tribunal, a loss of eligibility as a result of declaring an incorrect lustration statement, and a loss of eligibility as a result of being sentenced to a prison sentence for an intentional offence prosecuted by public prosecution. Polish law does not vary in this respect from regulations in other European democracies. In Poland there is no professional census.

7.3.2 Candidate registration procedures

Candidates for an MP might be proposed by institutions (party or "coalition" electoral committees) or voters themselves (electoral committees of voters). In the latter case they might be formed when 1000 citizens desire to do so by signing proper documentation and submitting it to the National Electoral Commission. Information on the candidate is limited to providing the public with their first and last names, their profession and place of residence. The order on a given electoral list is arranged by the committee. The number of candidates on the list must be no fewer than the number of MPs elected in a given constituency and no higher than twice the number.

According to the code, each gender must constitute at least 35% of the candidate pool on the electoral lists. DAP experts, while referring to this issue (the survey question was a request for an assessment of the existence of "equal possibilities of making use of the right to be elected"), assessed it as quite low – 5.1. This is much lower than the assessment results of other aspects of elections and the party system. Furthermore, one of the highest deviations of the standard assessment recorded is a demonstration of great incoherence in the assessment by the expert group. In other words this is a controversial issue. Experts believe that the ability to run for office is limited mainly by economic factors.

7.3.3 Candidate access to the electorate

No international agencies or projects assessing the functioning of democracy in Poland point at candidates' alleged problems with accessing the electorate. However, in reality the chances of candidates for a successful contact with the electorate are on the one hand shaped by their financial capabilities and on the other hand by their political position in the party or in the electoral committee.

DAP has determined that the successful communication of candidates with their electorate is limited mainly by financial resources. It must be stressed, however, that both Polish public opinion and numerous candidates poorly understand the results of "open" electoral lists in Polish electoral law. As a consequence, they fail to appreciate vast possibilities of bottom-up (outside-the-institution) organization of the candidate and voter relationship.

7.3.4 Candidate access to the media

The issue which is most widely debated is undoubtedly the role of the central media, especially the public ones including television, in "making them available" for particular candidates. The question of the division of airtime among numerous candidates running for president is especially controversial. This issue concerns not only airtime, since it might be managed, but also the so-called debates, which raise a lot of emotions. It cannot be denied that having a debate between a dozen or so candidates is a challenging – if at all possible –,task. On the other hand, an important pillar and indicator of the quality of liberal democracy tells us to take care of "weaker" candidates.

CBOS reports (BS/107/2010) concerning the assessment of the presidential campaign of 2010 shows that 53% of Poles watched that year the television debate between the two main candidates for the presidency. Out of that group, 33% watched both debates. Watching debates is strongly correlated with participation in the elections. 40% of the respondents are convinced of the political neutrality of public television but blaming television for favouring one candidate is related to the political affiliation of the respondents, even though among the undecided the percentage was also pretty high, amounting to 47%. Among the commercial television stations, the political independence of POLSAT was assessed higher than that of TVN.

The legislation envisions equal access to the public media for all candidates running for an MP office as well as the head of state's office. Regulations regard the time and the place in the media where free airtime is made available for the candidates.

Regardless of the generally positive evaluation of legal provisions, actual access to the media, especially the public ones, has been constantly criticized. It especially concerns the periods of electoral campaigns and the National Electoral Commission has repeatedly pointed this out. Important issue violating electoral law is the premature commencement of the electoral campaign, which is called "informative" by parties and allegedly not related to the elections. Another abuse of the starting time of the electoral campaign is that government politicians visit different parts of the country, which is presented as "providing on-the-spot-guidance." What is more, it happens to be reported by the media in a manner quite disproportionate to the actual importance of the event.

7.3.5 Neutrality of the public media in electoral campaigns

In short: the neutrality of the public media during the electoral campaigns happens to be defective. This problem cannot be solved because the media are diverse and political programs are hosted by various journalists. It also happens that for instance public television stations, in order to ensure pluralism not only of the political but also of the journalist nature, invites journalists of doubtful political neutrality to interview politicians. As a result we might face a similar situation to that of the presidential campaign in 2010 when one of the invited journalists, before asking the candidate a question, engaged in a several-minute-long tirade peppered with accusations and insinuations referring to that candidate.

7.4 Equality of the vote

7.4.1 Equality of the vote on the level of electoral law

On the level of legal regulations we face total equality of the right to vote except for age-related limitations we mentioned before and which are common in most countries. Temporary deprivation of the right to vote, whether related to one's mental health or criminal record, fundamentally does not depart from the regulations in other democracies.

7.4.2 Execution of the principle of the equality of the vote in practice

A simple mathematical calculation shows that every single one out of the 460 MPs in the Sejm represents approximately 82,090 Poles. Out of those, 66,716 Poles are entitled to vote. The need to adjust the borders of the constituencies to the administrative divisions of the state and the allocation of a natural number of mandates to every constituency results in the fact that the real number of inhabitants per 1 MP mandate ranges from 0.944 to 1.047 of the average. Due to the fact that big cities are characterized by a lower number of minors, the difference between the number of inhabitants and the number of voters is smaller than in rural areas. It means that differences in age structure double the differentiation of electoral representativeness: depending on the constituency there is 0.906 to 1.119 of the average number of voters per one mandate.

The above ranges are amplified because of the differences in the turnout. It is significantly higher in big urban centres. In the latest parliamentary elections the national record of participation was set in Warsaw and it was 69.44%, whereas the record low turnout was noted in Elblag and it was only 41.24%. As a consequence, if the range against the Polish average is measured by the number of real voters (not only those entitled to vote) it will increase to the range of 0.813 to 1.607 of the average. It means that during the current term of the Sejm every MP elected in Warsaw is representing twice the number of voters than an MP from the Elblag constituency: 51,849 persons against 26,234 persons. This is such a significant difference that it makes one wonder whether it does not breach the principle of equality of the vote, which is key for democracy.

Fig./Tab. 7.3: For every MP elected in October 2011 there are ...

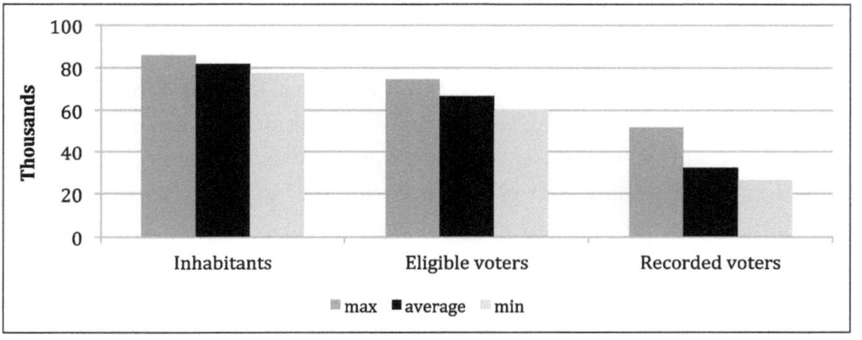

Source: PKW

In the case of Senate elections the equality of the vote is even more problematic. The difference is close to being fourfold in magnitude (hence twice as big as in the Sejm elections), which brings into question the representativeness of the Senate.

Fig./Tab. 7.4: For every senator elected in October 2011 there are ...

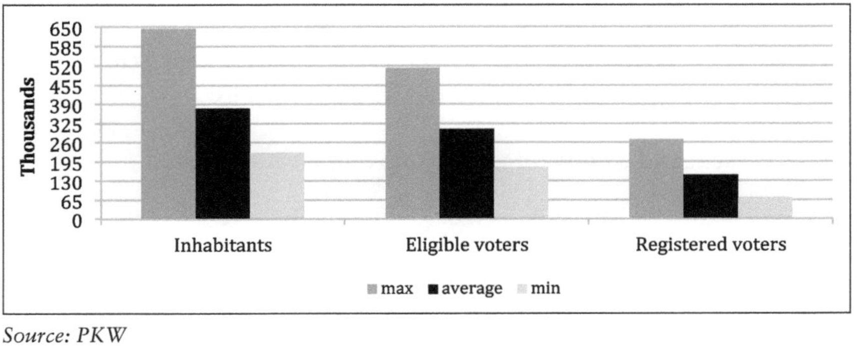

Source: PKW

7.5 Parliament structure versus social structure

The Parliament is, as a rule, a body representing the whole of society; therefore it is reasonable to expect that it will be representative for the society while constituting some kind of its "mirroring." It is to ensure a good quality of the representation and the execution of "the will of the people" as well as the "responsiveness" of the Parliament towards citizens' interests. Another issue is a rich diversity of methods in which this responsiveness and representativeness might be ensured. A classic approach to the question of representativeness assumes that it is most completely executed when the representatives are the same (or similar) as the ones they are to represent. There is also an alternative approach which assumes the functional ability (based on policy proximity) of representatives to properly fulfil the role of the representative regardless of whether they resemble their electorate or not (Pitkin 1967).

7.5.1 An analysis of legal procedures ensuring the presence of disadvantaged groups in the Parliament

Taking care of minority rights is one of the fundamental features of liberal democracy. The mechanism ensuring greater chances for the presence of minority groups is waiving the necessity of their electoral committees to cross a 5% threshold of the vote cast to participate in the division of MPs' mandates. In practice, owing to the small territorial dispersion of the other minorities, this privilege is enjoyed only by the German minority whose representatives have ceaselessly been present in the subsequent Sejm terms elected since 1991.

The new electoral law passed in 2011 supports the idea of more gender equality in representative body elections by requiring representatives of each sex to comprise at least 35 % of every electoral list.

7.5.2 Presence of disadvantaged groups on electoral lists

The electoral code determines the minimum percentage of individuals of each sex on electoral lists but the issue of their allocation is left for the parties to decide. At the same time women's organizations are calling for an alternative allocation of male and female candidates, which necessarily enforces parity on electoral lists. So far internal statute regulations concerning gender parity have been accepted only by one political party, namely *Twój Ruch* (Your Movement, formerly Palikot's Movement). The Civic Platform uses a solution resembling a zipper: for every top three candidates at least one place is assigned for a woman and two women for every top five candidates. The gender quota introduced into the new Electoral Code has resulted in a significant growth in the number of women on the lists.

In 2007, that is, in the latest Sejm elections, when the quotas were not in force, 20% of the candidates were women (in total on the list of the parties that made it to the Parliament), whereas this percentage on particular lists did not differ a great deal. In 2011 women constituted over 42%, including 44.5% on the list of Palikot's Movement (currently Your Movement) as well as 39.8% on the list of the Law and Justice (the National Electoral Commission's data).

The rules for placing candidates into particular spots on the lists are not quite clear; it remains unknown who makes the ultimate decision, neither is it known what criteria are taken into consideration by the parties while prioritizing their candidates (Przybysz 2012).

7.5.3 Presence of disadvantaged groups in the Parliament

The general number of women in the Polish parliament increased from 20.4% during the sixth term of the Sejm (2007- 2011) to 23.9% in the seventh term (after 2011). However, it must be noted that there is significant diversity between the parties: in the parliamentary club of Civic Platform women constitute over 1/3, whereas in the clubs of the Polish People's Party and Your Movement it is less than 1/10 of the members.

7.6 Participation and legitimacy of the authorities

7.6.1 Electoral turnout on the national and local level

The participation of Poles in political elections is very low, even when compared with other countries of Central and Eastern Europe. There has been a constancy since the beginning of the democratic opening, as in the "contract" elections on June 4th, 1989 when the turnout was only 62%, whereas in the other countries of the region in the first free elections the turnout as a rule was over 90%. During the whole period of the transformation the turnout has been on average less than 50%.

A slightly higher participation of Poles has been recorded in the presidential elections: 55% (the only exception is 2005 when in both rounds only approximately 50% of the entitled voters participated in the elections).

The Polish National Election Study (PGSW) data shows at the same time that exclusion from participation in Poland is neither structural nor permanent. It is difficult to indicate a particular social group that would be significantly underrepresented in the electoral process. Despite the fact that in every parliamentary or presidential elections approximately half of voters stay at home, there are only 20% of citizens who permanently decline from voting, which is more or less the same number as those who always vote. The majority vote occasionally: sometimes they do, sometimes they do not.

7.6.2 Acceptance of election results

During the whole transformation process since 1989 all actors of the Polish political arena have accepted election results except for obvious protests in particular constituencies, which had specific objections of a procedural, technical or logistic nature.

7.6.3 Citizens' interest in public activity on the local level

The level of civil activity in Poland is very low, as over 54% of the respondents have never participated in any kind of civil activities[66]. The level of engagement in any activities for the local community is also extremely low and the percentage of individuals who did not undertake any activity for the social community during the last year is 75%.

66 A study known as "*Current Issues and Events*" (268) conducted from September 5th to September 16th, 2012 on a representative sample of 985 adults resident in Poland.

Fig./Tab. 7.5: Have you been personally involved in any initiative of the local community? Please select all the activities that you have undertaken during the last 12 months

Co-organizing local events for the local community	9.1
Direct contact with an official in any matter related to the local community (apart from dealing with one's own business in the office)	7.7
Volunteering, doing unpaid work for the local community or an organization	6.4
Direct contact with a local councillor or a politician in or running for office	5.4
Working in a social organization or an NGO	4.3
Working in a church/parish organization (apart from participating in religious ceremonies)	4.1
Active participation in public consultation	3.9
Contacting the media to make them interested in a problem	2.4
No, none of the above	75.3

Source: CBOS/DAP – Pankowski 2013

7.7 Tripartite Commission

Mature democracies differ in terms of numerous issues. One of the more important features of this diversity is the scope of the de-commodification of human lot, i.e. situation in which individual's fortune is not dependent on sheer market forces alone. Methods of gaining this autonomy do differ but an important element is the scope of corporatist mechanisms introduced, where the so-called Tripartite Commissions play a key role.

7.7.1 Tripartite Commission activities

Since 1994 in Poland a conflict of interests between employers and employees has been resolved through social dialogue under the operation of the Tripartite Commission. Since 2003 the Tripartite Commission has operated under a legal framework (Dziennik Ustaw 2001 No. 100, item 1080).). In June 2013, the Tripartite Commission stopped its operations after the conflict between trade unions and the government.

Fig./Tab. 7.6: Assessment of the operation of the Tripartite Commission assembling representatives of employer organizations, trade unions and the government

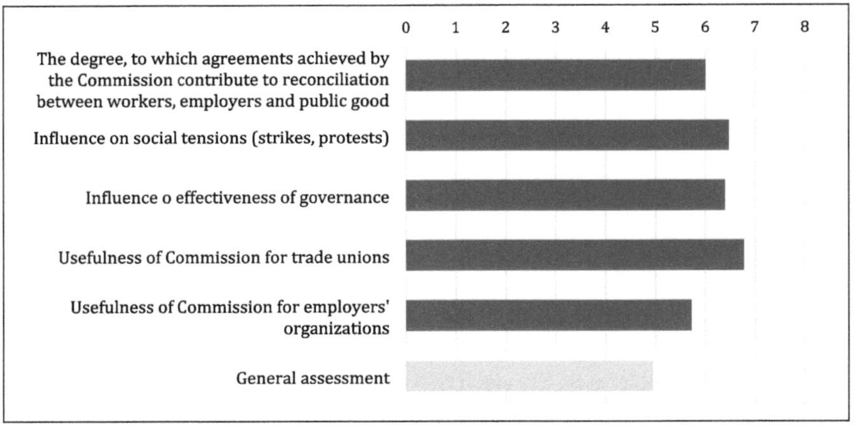

Source: DAP expert survey. Average on a scale from 0 to 10

The social assessment of the operation of the Tripartite Commission is shown in CBOS study conducted in December 2008. Unfortunately, no later data is at our disposal. At the end of 2008 knowledge about the operation of the Tripartite Commission was not common. Only 14% of the respondents stated that they had a grasp of the Commission's work. Out of those only 2% declared they knew more than the bare minimum. Half of the respondents (49%) had never heard of the Tripartite Commission before. To sum up the results of the CBOS study, it might be stated that Poles in 2008 were poorly acquainted with social dialogue and its institutions. Only a few respondents were acquainted with the negotiations taking place in the Tripartite Commission but they had poorly formulated opinions about the negotiation participants and their interests.

The Bertelsmann Transformation Index (BTI), in their report entitled *Policy Coordination*, allotted Poland 9.5 out of 10 points believing that, despite the tensions within the Tripartite Commission, the coordination of sectorial policies is running smoothly. At the same time it indicates that if someone was to blame for the low efficiency of the operation of the Commission, it would be rather the trade unions.

7.8 Summary

1. Polish electoral procedures and the institutions that organize them, despite some critical remarks, deserve some credit. This assessment does not differ from those of international organizations dealing with similar evaluations.
2. The electoral law and its practice must also be regarded as satisfactory, even though in this case many specific mechanisms and social habits should be revised. Public invention in terms of candidate registration and social "assistance" during voting is a worrying issue.
3. We must be critical of the performance of the media in the public sphere. Their role in election campaigns makes us formulate numerous critical remarks. It especially concerns commercial stations. However, what is especially worrying is the lack of political neutrality of the public media. At the same time the experience of the latest election campaigns of 2010 and 2011 seem to indicate some improvement in this matter.
4. The equality of the vote, even though legally secured, in reality deviates significantly from the assumed ideal. In a sense it does the same everywhere else and there seems to be a remedy of a double nature, namely: (a) changes in legal regulations, especially in drawing the borders of the constituencies or more reactive changes in assigning the number of mandates for a given constituency (b) on the citizens' side: taking more interest in public matters. The latter is especially rarely addressed; however, we clearly notice a great amount of apathy in Poles when it comes to numerous public matters, including political ones, from their absence at the polls to an unwillingness to take an interest in learning how the proportional system with "open lists" really works. Scholarly effort shows that it works pretty well provided citizens are active.
5. Other types of inequalities in access to voting, running for office or supporting candidates exist as well. Yet, some improvement in participation in the political process on the part of both women and individuals previously excluded for technical reasons is noted in recent years. There is however some room for further improvement in this area; it is equally a task for politicians, lawmakers and citizens. A change of political culture does not take place overnight and even the best legal regulations will not change the political reality immediately.

6. The foundation of the reliability of the elections and governance in democracy is the „responsiveness" of the authorities, that is, the ability to listen to citizens' preferences and respond accordingly. However, a „responsible" citizen is of no less value; whether he or she takes an interest in public matters, is a competent individual accurately assessing socio-political reality, and whether he or she is driven by public, not only private interests, matters a lot. Our analyses indicate that nostalgia for such a citizen in Poland is quite justified.

Bibliography

Dyktat czy uczestnictwo? Diagnoza partycypacji publicznej w Polsce [Dictate or Participation? A diagnosis of public participation in Poland], edited by A. Olech, vol. 1, Institute of Public Affairs, Warsaw 2012.

H. Pitkin, *The Concept of Representation*, University of California Press, Berkeley 1967.

D. Przybysz, *Analiza wyników wyborów parlamentarnych 2011* [An analysis of the results of parliamentary elections 2011], Institute of Public Affairs, Warsaw 2012 (the report has not been published).

D. Wąsik, *Przestępstwa przeciwko wyborom i referendum* [Offences against elections and referendums], volumina.pl, Olsztyn 2012.

8. Party system

"No party – no democracy." This motto is as real as it is incomplete since there are no non-democratic regimes that could do without parties. Political parties play numerous key public roles from socialization via integration and articulation to management. Parties are indispensable in democracies since they deal with social, economic and cultural life as a whole and they cannot afford to represent sectorial interests or focus exclusively on the distributive side of politics like, for instance, trade unions. Parties do not operate in a vacuum but are instead surrounded by numerous organizations, the key elements of this surrounding are the remaining parties of a party system.

The Polish situation for a long time deviated from the democratic standards in this regard as political parties would undergo constant changes; some would disappear, some would be established anew, others would split into two or more entities and relations between them could be defined with any term but "systemic." For a few years now, however, we have been dealing with clear institutionalization of the party system and stabilization of the parties (Markowski, Cześnik 2012).

8.1 Freedom of operation of political parties

8.1.1 Legal procedures concerning the operation of political parties

Polish parties operate in accordance with the bill of June 27th, 1997 on political parties (*Ustawa z dnia 27 czerwca 1997 r. o partiach politycznych*, Dziennik Ustaw 2011 No. 155, item 924). Every political party might make use of the envisioned rights after having been entered into the register of political parties. The law defines that "political parties shape their structures and the mode of operation in accordance with the principles of democracy, especially by ensuring transparency of those structures, appointment of the party body through elections and making decisions by the majority of the votes" (Art. 8).

8.1.2 Characteristics of Polish political parties

During the period of over two decades of democratic Poland, Polish parties were characterized by significant instability. During the last decade, however, this situation has changed considerably. The parties demonstrate a range of mature features, as stable and legitimized leadership and if a change in leadership occurs (as in the recent case of the Polish People's Party – PSL) it proceeds in accordance with the democratic procedures envisioned for leadership selection. Clear relations of either cooperation or competition between parties have improved too. In a survey from March 2012[67] respondents were asked to determine on a 7-point scale (from -3 to +3), to what extent each of the mentioned parties expresses their views and represents their interests (Cybulska 2012).

Fig. /Tab. 8.1: The level of party representativeness

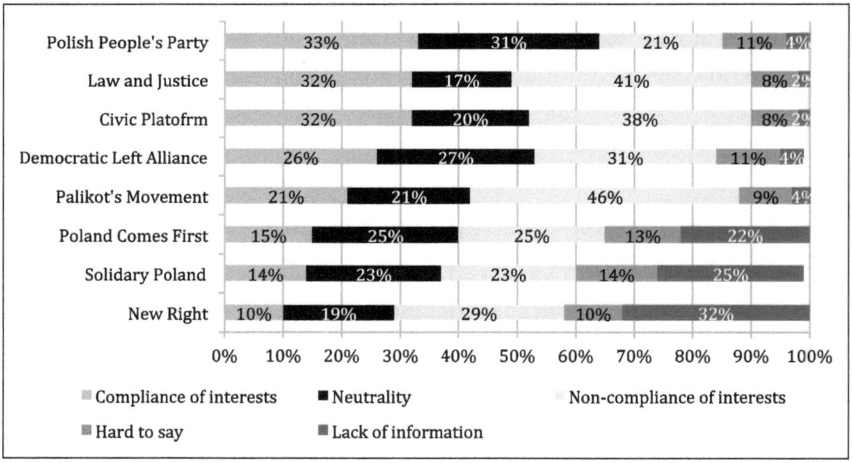

Source: CBOS – Cybulska 2012

67 A study entitled "*Current Problems and Events*" conducted from March 8th to March 14th 2012 on a representative sample of 1015 adults resident in Poland.

Fig./Tab. 8.2: Representativeness of political parties

	2007		2010		2012	
	Average	Standard deviation	Average	Standard deviation	Average	Standard deviation
PO	0.2	1.86	0.39	1.94	-0.33	1.87
PiS	-0.03	2.03	-0.45	2.14	-0.35	2.04
PSL	-0.15	1.41	0.08	1.52	0.15	1.15
SLD	-0.72	1.71	0.08	1.73	-0.28	1.6

Source: CBOS – Cybulska 2012

An analysis of the representativeness of political parties in recent years demonstrates a decrease of identification with PO (Civic Platform), PiS (Law and Justice) and SLD (Democratic Left Alliance). Representativeness has improved only in the case of PSL (Polish People's Party).

Fig./Tab. 8.3: Identification with political parties

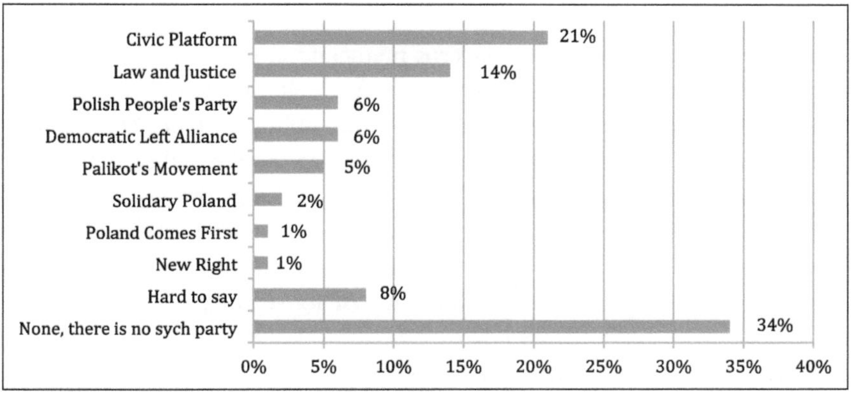

Source: CBOS – Cybulska, Pankowski 2013

A study[68] from March 2013 shows that slightly above half (56%) of respondents can point to the party which best fulfils their expectations (Cy-

68 A study entitled "*Current Issues and Events*" (272) conducted from January 1st to January 9th, 2013 on a representative sample of 1227 adults resident in Poland.

bulska, Pankowski 2013). Over 34% of Poles believe that there is no such a party while 8% have no opinion on the matter.

Fig./Tab. 8.4: Identification with political parties (changes over time)

Is there a political party in Poland that you perceive as:	2003	2006	2007	2008	2011	2013
close to you	39%	45%	33%	36%	36%	25%
a bit closer than others	14%	14%	13%	14%	64%	18%
there is no such a party	47%	41%	54%	50%	–	56%

Source: CBOS Cybulska, Pankowski 2013

8.1.3 Limitations to the freedom of operation of political parties

The fifth chapter of the bill from 1997 speaks of limitations to the freedom of operation of political parties. Most importantly, it states that, recognizing issues violating the provisions laid down in the Constitution with regard to the aims of political parties is in the competence of the Constitutional Court (Art. 42).

Freedom of operation also concerns financial matters as well as the issue of activities not envisaged in the party statute, including running a business. The law is crystal clear about the prohibition of political parties "performing tasks which are reserved in the legal regulations for public authority bodies;" they cannot replace those bodies (Art. 6). The provisions of the Constitution are final when it comes to limiting the freedom of operation of parties. Their infringement, similar to the case of other organizations and associations, might result in the prohibition of operation of a given organization.

8.2 Effectiveness of the party system

A retrospective overview of the development and performance of the Polish party system demonstrates that enormous changes have taken place in Poland in the last decade, which also concerns the years of 2012 – 2013, assessed by our project. Only in the last 7 years, as well as the years of 2012 – 2013 which we cover in detail, for the first time in the democratic history of Poland has the government coalition been permanent and the coalition contract written down and respected.

8.2.1 The ability of political parties to maintain a stable government coalition

Despite numerous program-related tensions and implemented policies, the coalition of PO (Civic Platform) and PSL (Polish People's Party) demonstrates significant durability and there are no reasons to expect it might break up. However, there have been plenty of impasses starting from the issue of agricultural social insurance, to the approach towards the reform of the retirement system and the reform of the health-care system, to the issues connected with particular provisions of budgetary expenditure. Therefore, apart from "positive" factors cementing the current coalition, we are also dealing with a structural "negative" element: the fear of losing access to power in the case of new elections.

8.2.2 Frequency of government changes in the period between elections

In the last two terms of the parliament session there have been no changes in the coalition configuration of the two partners: PO (Civic Platform) and PSL (Polish People's Party). The only changes were those formally or democratically envisaged, that is after the elections in 2011 a new government was appointed. A change of the Deputy Prime Minister has taken place, which was related to a change of the leader of one of the coalition parties.

8.3 Parties as organizations

Polish parties, similar to the majority of parties in the world, perform several fundamental functions: mobilization, socialization, recruitment, articulation of interests, and last but not least organization of the government once they come to power. Contemporary parties operating in the democratic order must be assessed precisely on the basis of the extent to which they fulfil these functions.

8.3.1 Internal procedures of parties

Issues related to internal democracy of political parties appear in the following bills: in accordance with article 11 of the Polish Constitution, the essence of political parties is influencing through democratic methods the state politics; article 8 of the bill on political parties (Dziennik Ustaw 1997

No. 98, item 604) indicates that "political parties shape their structures and rules of operation in accordance with the principles of democracy." The legal framework defining the existence of democracy in Polish political parties is however general and not clear, which is why the law in this respect needs to be amended (Chmaj 2011, p. 13).

Why do parties need internal democracy?

A multitude of arguments could be quoted in favour of the necessity to obey democratic procedures within political parties, which is thoroughly discussed in the publication entitled *On Democracy in Polish Political Parties.* Indeed, parties in their statutes demonstrate that the decision-making process within them is in accordance with democratic procedures. However, the practice observed as a result of the ISP (Institute of Public Affairs) studies is different: parties live off state subsidies. Hence, they are not private organizations that may, independently of other factors, establish their own internal order. A party has a socializing function towards its political activists while operating within the party, its members develop habits and ideas relevant for the general political activity. It is important since in the public institutions, which are influenced by parties and party activists, individuals are required to act in accordance with democratic rules. As a consequence – the argument goes - a democratic training within party organization is an important basis for subsequent activity within administrative bodies. Analyses concerning the internal democracy of parties were conducted in 2011 and concerned the parties of the Sejm term of 2007 – 2011. No response was received from two parties: PiS (Law and Justice) refused to participate in this study without giving any reason; SLD (Alliance of the Democratic Left) ignored the study. According to the report, quote, "it is difficult to talk about a healthy practice that meets democratic standards of a party's functioning if there is no possibility to control it. Parties having all the characteristics of public organizations should not behave like private and hermetic companies hiding from public opinion the secrets of their activities" (p. 55).

8.4 Financing political parties

8.4.1 Legal mechanisms

The fourth chapter of the bill from 1997 consists of dozens of articles, which constitute approximately half of the total. The Polish lawmakers are extremely detailed in this matter and do not only define very precisely what constitutes party assets (Art. 24), but also indicate in a detailed manner from where a party might derive income (for instance from the sale of assets, loans, etc.); it also unambiguously defines what a political party cannot do (for instance carrying out public fundraising). Parties must be supported exclusively by Polish citizens and the amount acquired must also be clearly specified. The amount of subsidies received by parties that obtained a particular percentage of votes nationwide is described algorithmically. The rules for a situation in which two parties merge or split are also very clearly defined (Art.31), as well as a method for preparing the annual financial report on all subsidies and expenditures (Art. 34).

8.4.2 Law implementation

Financing election campaigns

The following problems connected with financing election campaigns seem to be frequent:

A. Election pre-campaign. Conducting – in a covert way – electioneering for particular individuals and groups during the period preceding commencement of the campaign is a problem. In the case of the pre-campaign carried out by other entities "it constitutes a problem to prove that these activities aim at promoting a particular candidate or groups running for office, or potentially anti-opponent activity (a negative campaign)." This problem is described by the National Electoral Commission (PKW) *(A report on implementation of the bill from January 5th 2011: the Electoral Code for the Sejm and Senate elections of the Republic of Poland conducted on October 9th, 2011)*. According to the National Electoral Commission, the regulations contain significant gaps that do not allow it to punish this type of behaviour. A pre-campaign may be conducted in various ways in the form of informative, social and entertainment actions[69].

69 Transparency of financing election campaigns and political parties – ISP 2012, p. 8.

On the other hand, however, it must be remembered that a too restrictive prohibition of political promotion during the period before the election campaign may gravely breach the principles of freedom of speech.

B. A "gray economy" in financing election campaign, created by unauthorized entities already in the course of its formal procedure. It usually takes the form of misusing public offices occupied by candidates running in the election campaign. It is often difficult to indicate which behaviour constitutes misuse of office. Analyses of ISP experts aimed at removing these perils lead to the formulation of the following recommendations: introducing into the Electoral Code regulations regarding the election pre-campaign and sanctions for entities conducting it; complementing the control system exercised by the National Electoral Commission with monitoring procedures for the process of financing elections already in the course of the campaign process; an increase in human resources at the disposal of the National Electoral Commission; limiting for the election campaign duration the possibility of distributing materials financed by public institutions where public officials are running for an office; creating conditions for effective operating of relevant NGOs and the media that undertake the task of monitoring the finance of electoral campaigns in Poland; activating mechanisms of social control; increasing the openness of the competent authorities towards reporting irregularities.

C. Reporting by election committees participating in elections

Election committees are bound to issue reports, which is the key element of the financial transparency of the election campaign; however, in this field certain problems occur.

- Releasing materials on the Internet; according to the National Electoral Commission, election committees did not always fulfil these duties.
- Submitting objections to the financial reports of election committees. Objections might be submitted by political parties and election committees that took part in that particular election as well as associations and foundations that in their statutes envisage actions related to a financial analysis of election campaigns. The first problem is that objections may only be submitted during the 30 days after the election. This is quite a

short term. Secondly, it is unreasonable to limit a circle of institutions entitled to submit objections.

- Publishing financial reports in a quite general form. The National Electoral Commission publishes the financial reports of election committees but the document contains only the main categories of the expenditures and revenues of election committees.

Recommendations: (a) imposing sanctions for the failure to create a website by an election committee; (b) prolonging the deadline for submitting objections; (c) abolishing limitations for types of entities that might submit objections to the financial reports; (d) facilitating access to the source material (bills, invoices).

D. Sanctions for breaching the provisions for financing the campaign

A nominated financial officer is responsible for the finances of an election committee. A written agreement for any financial liability is necessary. The Electoral Code provides for the financial and criminal liability of their financial nominee for incurring liabilities for the election committee. This is a pretty heavy burden and election committees have the problem of finding individuals willing to undertake this task.

There are no clear regulations concerning the handing over of "non-monetary value" to election committees. The only legally acceptable form of handing over "non-monetary value" is distributing posters and leaflets by natural persons. The National Electoral Commission also notes that the term "non-monetary value" has to be defined more clearly.

Recommendations: (a) widening the catalogue of non-monetary value that is not subject to sanctions that fits the voluntary work formula, which will contribute to an increase in the civil activity of voters; (b) defining "non-monetary value;" (c) imposing less severe sanctions for financial nominees; (d) preparing an online course for financial nominees.

E. Financing political parties

Publishing information on party expenditures is a problem as well. The expenditures are published in Monitor Polski[70] in accordance with a special form. The applied mechanism is faulty: the multimillion zloty expendi-

70 Official journal containing internal regulations of state institutions.

tures of the parties are veiled in unclear general categories; the classification of expenditures is quite informal and optional.

Currently, the control of expenditures from subsidies is carried out exclusively in relation to financial and accounting issues. It would be advisable to include in the supervision mechanism the substance of party expenditures as well as verification of the conclusion of contracts of mandate also based on merits. The other problem is related to the social control of party expenditures, as documentation regarding operations on appropriations from subsidies is in the party's headquarters and access to it is limited. The objections formulated by social organizations and parties in relation to the information submitted by other political parties require additional regulation. Currently, there are no mechanisms enabling reliable preparation of objections: entities that could formulate objections have no (or limited) access to the financial documentation of political parties.

8.5 Parties in the Parliament

8.5.1 The position and activity of opposition parties in the parliament

Fulfilling the role of an opposition party in the parliament in Poland leaves a lot to wish for. Even though the customary leadership of the selected Sejm commissions is chaired by politicians of opposition parties, the overall influence of opposition parties is significantly limited. The first reason for this being the case is the fact that the government coalition wishes to, and in fact does, implement its own plans. The second reason is that being in the opposition in Poland is treated by opposition parties as time devoted to preparations aimed at winning the next elections.

The activity of opposition parties is far from responsible, usually characterized by emotional criticism rather than by submitting substantive policy proposals, coupled with spreading unrealistic promises. As a consequence we are dealing with a group that is fuelling up the electorate's expectations, which in the long term leads to growing frustration, political cynicism, and apathy of the electorate.

8.5.2 The scope for applying party discipline in the parliament

The issue of imposing so-called party discipline in parliamentary voting in many countries contributes to heated discussions. In Poland this situation is no different since the Constitution of the Republic of Poland states that "MPs are representatives of the Nation" not of their parties; neither are they bound by instructions from voters. An MP should always decide based on his/her own judgment.

Recently, that is in March 2013, CBOS conducted a study on Poles' opinions concerning the issue of imposing party discipline in parliamentary voting (BS/48/2013). According to the study, the majority (57%) is in favour of the statement that "during voting in the parliament, it is most important that MPs from the government coalition are in line with their own conscience, even if their vote is against agreed upon decisions taken by parties' headquarters, and contribute to the paralyzes of government's work." This percentage is 5 points higher than in a similar study conducted in 2000. Among the factors facilitating support for independence of MPs voting, the key factor is Poles' religiousness; among the most frequent churchgoers 70% are in favour of one exercising one's own judgment in deciding how to vote. It is also important to note that Poles significantly differ in relation to imposition of the party discipline, depending on the issues at stake.

8.6 Elections and the Polish party system: constitutive features

The shape and dynamics of party systems depend on numerous factors: the constitutional provisions, the electoral system, the socio-political divide in a given society or obviously the results of elections. In this chapter we will deal only with the relation between parliamentary elections (and only the latest ones from 2011) and the features of the party system as well as the logic of its cooperation and competition.

8.6.1 The elections of 2011

The latest parliamentary elections in 2011 have several specific features. For the first time in the democratic history of Poland after 1989, the mandate of the government coalition was renewed and the incumbents remained more or less the same if we view it through the prism of its composition. Secondly, they were regular elections that took place after a full four-year parliamentary cycle. Thirdly, these elections proved to numerous sceptics that the Polish party system is not "frozen." A completely new party made it into the Parliament – it managed to receive over 10% of the votes cast. The fourth feature is that the year of 2011 was the fourth year of the deep economic crisis in the world with which Poland had been dealing unexpectedly well. The fifth feature is that the elections took place in an atmosphere of deep social division due significantly, though not only, to the temporal proximity of the catastrophe in Smolensk. Few changes to the Electoral Code were introduced, as a consequence single-member constituencies were introduced to the Senate elections as well as diverse types of support for voting (for instance, the limited ability for casting a vote through a representative or via mail) and a change in voting hours (Skotnicki 2011).

8.6.2 The "shape" and dynamics of the party system

There is a range of commonly recognized indicators at our disposal that allow us to describe and assess the condition of our party system. Performing a diachronic comparison of the indicators allows for a better understanding of what happened on October 9th, 2011.

Fig./Tab. 8.5: Indicators of the Polish political system of 1991–2011

Indicator	1991	1993	1997	2001	2005	2007	2011
Fractionalization	0.93	0.90	0.78	0.78	0.83	0.70	0.73
Effective number of parties (Laakso & Taagepera 1)	13.86	9.80	4.59	4.50	5.86	3.32	3.74
Effective number of parties (Laakso & Taagepera 2)	10.45	3.88	2.95	3.60	4.63	2.82	3.00
Proportionality (Gallagher's indicator)	4.14%	15.74%	9.75%	4.42%	5.61%	4.39%	5.67%
Percentage of "wasted votes"	8.37%	34.44%	12.41%	9.37%	10.93%	4.12%	4.12%
Sum of two largest parties (votes)	24.31%	35.81%	60.96%	53,.2%	51.13%	73.62%	69.07%

Sum of two largest parties (mandates)	26.52%	65.87%	79.35%	61.09%	61.96%	81.52%	79.13%
Ratio of two largest parties (votes)	1.03	1.32	1.25	3.24	1.12	1.29	1.31
Ratio of two largest parties (mandates)	1.03	1.29	1.22	3.32	1.14	1.26	1.32

Source: own calculations on the basis of the PKW data

No less important than the above "static" features of the party system are their "dynamic" parameters, i.e. changes taking place from one election to another. Such a fundamental indicator of the stability of the party system is its "volatility," an aggregated measurement of voters' support for a particular party.

Fig./Tab. 8.6: Electoral instability of 1991–2011

Aggregated	**1991–1993**	**1993–1997**	**1997–2001**	**2001–2005**	**2005–2007**	**2007–2011**
Global	34.78%	19.19%	49.30%	38.39%	24.96%	13.74%
Inter-block	18.90%	7.58%	18.72%	26.16%	11.06%	2.36%
Individual	1991–1993	1993–1997	1997–2001	2001–2005	2005–2007	2007–2011
Inter-party	–	62.26%	55.94%	62.64%	34.48%	23.12%
Inter-block	–	15.47%	20.24%	27.69%	15.36%	17.24%

Source: own calculations on the basis of the PKW and PGSW

The data shown above allow us to make the convincing statement that in the last decade, especially in the elections (or after the elections) in 2011 the Polish party system indicates significant features of stability. It is reflected in the following: low electoral volatility, a negligible percentage of wasted votes, as well as the small disproportionality of translating the votes into strength for the party in the Parliament, and the high proportion of votes supporting the two largest parties of the system.

8.6.3 Relations between electorates

In multiparty systems like the one in Poland we are dealing with quite complex relations between the parties. They are more chaotic in young democracies than in stable democracies and it is exactly their predictability that is one of the fundamental indicators of the institutionalization of the party system (Mainwaring, Scully 1995).

A dominant role in this regard is played by party elites and their decision-making groups, but citizens' feelings or the preferences of voter groups in relation to political entities such as parties cannot be underestimated.

The tradition of the Polish National Election Study allows us to recreate effective relations towards particular parties: on an 11-point scale where one end means the maximum level of liking and the other full aversion, every respondent has the option of commenting on whether they like or dislike (and its intensity) each political party. Such a battery of questions was asked in the 2011 elections as well. Respondents were indicating if and to what extent they liked the following 5 parties: PO (Civic Platform), PiS (Law and Justice), RP (Palikot's Movement), SLD (Democratic Left Alliance) and PSL (Polish People's Party).

Let's start from an overview of the results relevant to all Poles (details – see Markowski, Cześnik 2012). In doing so, we should first consider the most obvious issues. All Poles like PO the most (average 5.11), which is hardly surprising since this party won the elections and has the highest number of supporters. Next, one should expect (in accordance with the above logic) that the second party (PiS) in terms of size of voters support, which had only a slightly worse result than the winner but much better than the remaining three parties, will enjoy the second best level of affection among Poles. This is however not the case, as Law and Justice, whose average result was 3.36, stands on fourth position behind such parties as PSL and SLD that have three times fewer supporters. Additionally, the results for those who do not vote show exactly the same hierarchy (the ratio of mutual relationship is slightly different though) as in the case of Poles in general, namely: Poles like PO the most and PiS the least. Those who do not vote, similar to all Poles, are not very keen on the major opposition party, that is, PiS. Thirdly, if we put together all of the affective assessments of the "remaining" four parties (except for one's own, which shows that a given electorate is ready to accept coalitions with other parties), the following picture emerges: the electorate of PiS likes all the other parties least (average 2.38), and this is the result which "categorically" deviates from the rest. The SLD electorate, in turn, is the most eager to accept the other parties. The party, which is least liked by the other electorates, is PiS (with one exception being that the least preferred party of PSL's electorate is RP).

Fig./Tab. 8.7: An assessment of the fondness for another party's electorate

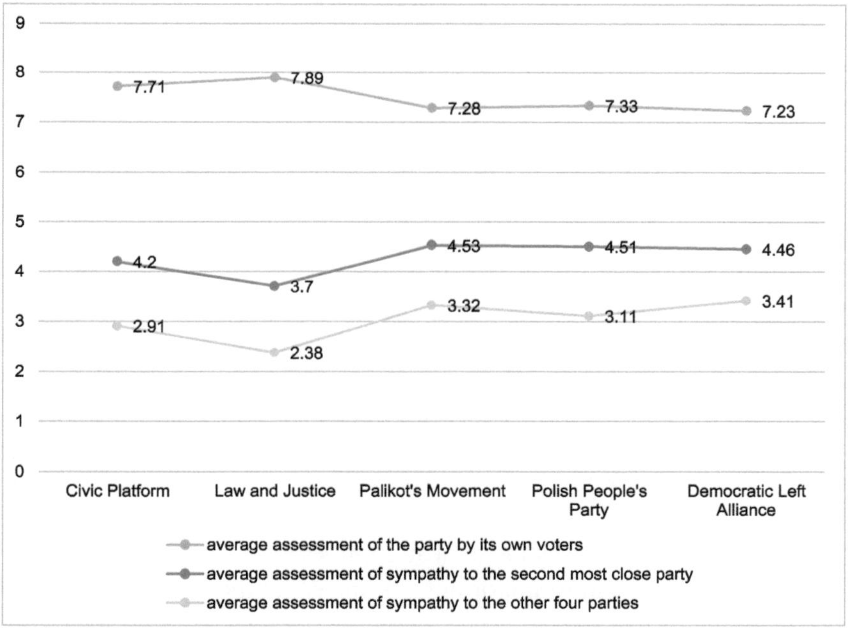

Source: Markowski, Cześnik 2012

The presented drawing indicates clearly that the electorate of PiS is quite different from the others; it is somehow lonely in a double sense: it dislikes all the other parties and adores most its own.

In conclusion, it is worth stressing the following phenomena (while taking into consideration the fact that a new parliamentary entity has emerged, which is important for many indicators presented in the tables above). Let's look through them one by one.

The fractionalization index measures the coherence of the party system; the lower its value, the more coherent the system is. This index slightly increased between 2007 and 2011 (from 0.70 to 0.73). Both indicators of the effective number of parties look similar – both its versions measured on the basis of the votes cast and the number of seats in the Parliament obtained by particular parties. When compared to 2007 these indicators have increased. Gallagher's index, which measures the disproportionality of the obtained parliamentary configuration in relation to the preferences of the sovereign, reveals that this indicator increased and exceeded the level from the last three elections (2001, 2005 and 2007). This is probably the result of the emergence of a new party or perhaps also to some extent a different type of dispersion of votes. A significant feature and the one, which shows the maturity of the party system and citizens, is the indicator of the percentage of wasted votes. It indicates the quality of the political elites, clarity of the signals sent by them to voters, and the latter's ability to accurately read them. This indicator manifests voters' ability of rational calculation and a reliable estimation of the chances of small parties. Let's note that in 2011 the percentage of wasted votes was identical to that from four years before, which, when taking into consideration the emergence of a new political party and differences in electoral participation, as well as an increase in the disproportionality and fractionalization of the system, speaks well of the increasing qualifications of the Polish voter. In other words, looking back to 1993, the Polish voter now has a better understanding of the real power of political parties and in comparison with that year they are currently wasting almost 10 times fewer votes.

Finally, one of the most important parameters of the party system is the electoral volatility of the electorate (compare Cześnik, Markowski 2004), both the aggregated level measured with the so-called Pedersen index, and the individual level recreated on the basis of Polish voters' preferences unveiled by PGSW (Polish National Electoral Study). The most important indicator is presented in the "global volatility" row, and for the period that compares the results of the last two elections, the value is 13.7%. This is the lowest value since the beginning of the transformation. The observed tendency is strongly confirmed in the individual-level data between 2001 and 2011, as we have recorded a decrease of individual volatility from 62.6% to 23.1%.

The above comment needs to be supplemented with the results of a more detailed analysis of transfers between the main political parties from the parliamentary elections in 2007 and 2011 based on exit-poll data (details – see Markowski, Cześnik 2012).

Out of the PO electorate, over 80% constitute loyal voters who voted for this party in both elections (their number might be estimated at 4,600,000 voters). The other largest group in this electorate from 2011 are individuals who did not vote in 2007 and those who did not remember how they voted that year (they might be estimated at 275,000-300,000 voters). While taking into consideration how heated the dispute between the main protagonists of Polish politics is, a group of "overtaken" voters of PiS from 2007 is quite large and it might be estimated at slightly over 150,000 voters. The other groups are smaller. When it comes to the electorate of PiS this picture is quite similar. Its main part, also almost 80%, constitutes loyal voters: their number might be estimated at almost 3,400,000 voters. There are over 200,000 new voters in this electorate, and an additional approximately 270,000 voters who did not remember how they voted in 2007. The number of PO voters from 2007 who voted for PiS in 2011 is worth noting; this number is estimated more or less at 230,000. Let's add that this somehow prestigious duel for encouraging a larger number of the former voters of the main opponent is won primarily by PiS. This party is able to encourage more supporters of PO. The electorate of the new party RP (Palikot's Movement) consists mostly of the former voters of PO (half of this electorate). There is also a large group of individuals who have not voted so far (approximately 250,000 voters). Among PSL voters, the loyal ones constitute a dominant portion but there are also large groups of former supporters of PO and PiS.

In turn, among the electorate of SLD the largest group is undoubtedly composed of the voters of LiD (Left and Democrats) from 2007 but there is also a large group of former PO voters. In the case of both of these blocks the new voters are marginal. These results differ from those from 2007 (compare Markowski, Cześnik 2011, p. 118). At that time, in the electorates of both dominant parties, new voters constituted a significant part. Currently, among PO and PiS voters, the faithful constitute a dominant portion. This is further proof of the progressive consolidation of the system.

8.7 Summary

1. The Polish party system after years of chaos is demonstrating sings of consolidation. This process is facilitated both by the new Electoral Code, which is more pro-institutional, and the socialization of the electorate. The latter especially seems not to be overestimated as Poles have learned their party system and know what to expect from it.
2. The Polish party system is at the same time far from "freezing," a label offered by numerous political commentators so emotionally and with a high dose of ignorance. As Janusz Palikot proved, it is enough to comprehensively read the political preferences of Poles, and use some energy and media to become the third largest parliamentary club.
3. The above positively assessed structural transformation of the Polish party system cannot overcome the elements of its imperfection. Therefore, the electoral turnout of Poles remains low, (even though structural exclusions have not been recorded), party identification is low, and the quality of parties' representativeness could be higher. Low confidence in institutions and political elites is alarmingly high.
4. The method of financing political parties remains a serious problem. We devoted plenty of space to this issue because of its complexity. In our opinion, numerous recommendations should be legalized as soon as possible and end tested in the everyday operation of political parties. In this matter there are no ideal solutions. One should also not be fooled into thinking that bad practices in this field would soon be uprooted. In a broad perspective it all depends on us: citizens and politicians whose awareness of the universality of threats should prompt supervision and a response to bad practices.

Bibliography

O demokracji w polskich partiach politycznych [On democracy in Polish political parties], edited by M. Chmaj, M. Waszak, J. Zbieranek, Institute of Public Affairs, Warsaw, 2011.

Mechanizmy demokratyczne w polskich partiach politycznych. Opinie i rekomendacje [Democratic mechanisms in Polish political parties, opinions and recommendations], edited by J. Zbieranek, Institute of Public Affairs, Warsaw 2012.

Przejrzystość Finansowania Kampanii Wyborczych i Partii Politycznych. Wybrane Problemy i Rekomendacje [Transparency of Financing Election Campaigns and Political Parties. Selected Problems and Recommendations], M Gałązka, M. Solon-Lipiński, J. Zbieranek, Institute of Public Affairs, Warsaw 2012.

M. Cześnik, R. Markowski, *Uwarunkowania budowy polskiego systemu partyjnego: instytucje i procesy* [Conditions of creating the Polish party system: institutions and processes], in: *Budowanie instytucji państwa – w poszukiwaniu modelu 1989–2001* [Building the state institution – searching for the model 1989–2001], edited by I. Jackiewicz, Sejm Publishing House, Warsaw 2004, p. 25–47.

Diagnoza społeczna 2009. Warunki i jakość życia Polaków [A Social Diagnosis 2009. Conditions and the quality of life of Poles], edited by J. Czapiński, T. Panek, Social Monitoring Council, the University of Finance and Management in Warsaw, Warsaw 2009.

M. Cześnik, M. Kotnarowski, *Nowy wymiar politycznego współzawodnictwa: Polska solidarna versus Polska liberalna* [A new dimension of political rivalry: united Poland versus liberal Poland], "Political Studies" 2011, No.27, p. 129–158.

A. Cybulska, *Reprezentatywność partii politycznych* [Representativeness of Political Parties], CBOS report 2012. Available online on: http://www.cbos.pl/SPISKOM.POL/2012/K_056_12.PDF (accessed on 10.3.2013).

A. Cybulska, K. Pankowski, *O postępującej alienacji partii politycznych* [On progressing alienation of political parties], CBOS report 2012. Available online on: http://www.cbos.pl/SPISKOM.POL/2013/K_026_13.PDF (accessed on 12.3.2013).

R. Markowski, M. Cześnik, *Wybory parlamentarne 2007 roku – ciągły zamęt czy utrwalenie nowego rozłamu?* [Parliamentary Elections in 2007 – constant chaos or consolidation of a new divide?], "Studia Polityczne" 2011, No.27, p. 109–127.

Idem, *Wybory parlamentarne 2011 roku – kontynuacja i zmiana* [Parliamentary Elections in 2011 – a continuation and a change], "Studia Polityczne" 2012, No. 28.

A. Roberts, *Hyperaccountability: Economic voting in Central and Eastern Europe*, "Electoral Studies" 2008, No. 27, p. 533–546.

G. Sartori, *Parties and Party Systems. A Framework for Analysis*, Cambridge UP, Cambridge: 1976.

Kodeks wyborczy. Wstępna ocena [The Electoral Law. Preliminary Assessment], edited by K. Skotnicki, Sejm Publishing House, Warsaw 2011.

Money, Politics, Power: Corruption Risks in Europe, Transparency International, Berlin 2012.

Wybory do Parlamentu Europejskiego 2009. Monitoring finansów wyborczych [European Union Parliamentary Elections 2009. Monitoring of electoral finances], edited by A. Sawicki, Stefan Batory Foundation, Warsaw 2010;

G. Kopińska, J. Kucharczyk, A. Sawicki, M. Solon-Lipiński, M. Walecki, *Wybory prezydenckie 2005. Monitoring finansów wyborczych* [Presidential Elections 2005. Monitoring of electoral finances], edited by J. Zbieranek, Stefan Batory Foundation, Warsaw 2006.

9. Public responsibility and accountability of politicians

A key feature of democracy is accountability of politicians before citizens and the possibility to hold them responsible for their actions. Moreover, politicians operating within one type of institution should be subject to control of a different type, similarly to the way the executive should be controlled by the parliament. The first point of our analyses in this chapter concerns this type of dependency, i.e. controlling and holding the executive accountable by the parliament.

In the next section we discuss monitoring of public expenditures. Every year Poland spends hundreds of billions of Polish zlotys; in 2012 public expenditure totalled 680 billion PLN (Forum Obywatelskiego Rozwoju [Civil Development Forum] 2013). A significant part of those resources is spent on retirement and disability pensions, and related allowances. Expenditure on administrative management, education and higher education, roads, the armed forces, and the police cover the significant part of the remainder. Spending such large sums of money coming from taxpayers' pockets ought to be subject to citizen control.

Access of citizens to public information is necessary in order to be able to hold politicians accountable for their activities. This issue is touched upon in the last section of this chapter. Access to public information requires, first of all, appropriate legal regulations. Actual possibility to access public information is also discussed.

The data used in this chapter come from our own expert survey, reports by other organizations, and analyses of the content of existing legislature.

9.1 Scope and effectiveness of control and holding the executive accountable by the legislature

One of the constitutive features of democratic government is a parliament effectively controlling the executive. This process requires the existence of appropriate legal mechanisms and their proper application. Effective functioning of parliamentary commissions and the quality of MP questions and interpellations are as vital as the quality of government responses.

9.1.1 Legal mechanisms regulating the scope of government control by the parliament

In accordance with Art.95 of the Polish Constitution "the Sejm shall exercise control over the activities of the Council of Ministers within the scope specified by the provisions of the Constitution and statutes." The control covers the Council of Ministers and the government administration (Art.146, paragraph 3 of the Constitution of the Republic of Poland). The Parliament is entitled to collect information and assess the government while the government and its subunits are obliged to share information, take a position, etc. Examples of control mechanisms at the Sejm's disposal are: interpellations, parliamentary questions or committees of inquiry.

In accordance with Art.115.1 of the Constitution, the Prime Minister and particular ministers shall furnish answers to interpellations and MPs' questions. In addition to this, (Art.115.2 of the Constitution of the Republic of Poland) these entities shall furnish answers to matters raised in the course of each sitting of the Sejm. The response shall be submitted in writing within 21 days. In case of lack of response, or when the response is not satisfactory, the interested party may refer to the Speaker requesting additional explanation.

Commissions of inquiry are "extraordinary control measures launched in case of significant matters that require collecting information from a number of entities" (Art.11 of the Constitution of the Republic of Poland; the bill from January 21st 1999 on the Sejm committee of inquiry [*Ustawa z dnia 21 stycznia 1999 r. o sejmowej komisji Śledczej*, Dziennik Ustaw 2009 No.151, item 1218, amended in: Dziennik Ustaw 2010 No. 182, item 1228]).

Committees of inquiry are appointed by the majority of the Sejm. The composition of the committee should reflect the structure of the caucuses, which have their representatives in the Council of Seniors. Every individual invited to appear before the committee of inquiry is obliged to appear and make a statement. The committee may also refer to the Prosecutor General with a request to carry out specific operations.

9.1.2 Parliamentary questions, interpellations, requests and the quality of responses

According to DAP experts, as a rule MPs make proper use of available means for getting information and explanation. The average assessment of the quality of interpellations and MPs' questions was 6.4. The substantive content of the government response is evaluated slightly worse. Average assessment of the quality of the reaction and the content of the government response to interpellations and MPs' questions was 5.7.

9.1.3 Performance of parliamentary commissions

The effectiveness of government control by the Sejm commissions is assessed relatively poor. The average rating is 4.85. Negative evaluation of the performance of the Sejm commissions relates to the primacy of the executive over the legislature; the commissions are controlled by the Sejm majority and, because of this, they tend to be deprived of real subjectivity. Secondly, according to the experts, MPs are sometimes insufficiently competent and therefore often unable to accomplish meaningful evaluation. In this context lobbyists frequently take advantage of the poor competence of the commission members and effectively enforce desired legislation.

9.1.4 Scope and effectiveness of executive accountability at the local level

At the local (municipality) level there clearly is a problem related to effective control of the executive by the legislative body; "the dominance of the executive" prevails (Bober 2013). In 2002 the bill on the municipal government (*Ustawa o samorządzie gminnym*) introduced direct elections of the executive in municipalities. This contributed to strengthening the role of the executive while simultaneously weakening the control function exercised by the legislature. In the report entitled *Increasing dysfunctions, fundamental dilemmas, necessary actions* (Bober 2013) several key aspects of dominance of the executive in municipalities are pointed out. The only step that the municipal council can undertake in order to dismiss a mayor is to adopt a law on holding a referendum on his/her dismissal. Current legal mechanisms make it difficult for councils to dismiss incumbent mayor in office. First of all, a referendum must take place with turnout threshold required for its validity; secondly, the majority of votes cast should be in favour of dismissal. What is more, in case of dismissal caused by other reasons than failure to grant budgetary discharge, the council, by holding a referendum, risks early election. Another problem is the weakness of bodies that exercise control of the executive in everyday local practice. Council commissions have limited control possibilities. Councillors have no resources to commission expert opinions. Moreover, councils have no financial resources to make mayors execute the adopted bills. They also have minimal impact on the most important bill, i.e. the bill on the adoption of the budget, as it may only be presented by the executive body. Previously, before the regulations were changed, municipality councils had exercised control over the legislation using for this purpose audit and other committees of the council. However, "the possibilities of expressing real opposition to the executive body are very limited" (Bober 2013, p. 29).

In conclusion to this part we need to point that abilities to exercise control of the executive by the legislature on the municipal level are very limited. Weak position of councillors "causes a decay of local social participation" (Bober 2013, p. 29).

9.2 Control of public expenditure: central and local levels

A crucial aspect of public responsibility and accountability of politicians is control of public expenditure. Experts' opinion on the process of creation of the state budget is moderately positive. Transparency of this process (rating of 6.2 on a scale from 0 to 10 where 0 means complete lack of transparency) and control of implementation process of the budget (rating of 6.1) were rated the most favourably. Clarity of the presentation of the state budget (rating of 5.6) and transparency of its implementation (rating of 5.4) were assessed slightly lower.

The data regarding control of public expenditure other than the state budget is presented in the report on the audit of contracts co-financed from the EU funds. It was carried out by the President of the Public Procurement Office (Public Procurement Office 2013). In 2012, 232 audits were conducted. In 148 cases (close to 2/3) no breaches were recorded, whereas in 84 cases (over 1/3) violations of the bill on public procurement

(*Ustawa Prawo zamówień publicznych*) occurred. It needs to be stressed that the vast majority of tender procedures (142 cases) with no record of breaches are the largest tender procedures, i.e. their value is at least 10m euro for supplies and at least 20m euro for construction works. Comparing 2012 audit results with the ones from previous years there is improvement, as there is a visible increase in the proportion of cases without irregularities. In 2010, in 48% of cases there were no breaches of the provisions of the bill on public procurement; in 2011 this outcome was 58%, whereas in 2012 it was 64%.

On the other hand, in the subsequent years the percentage of cases where the recorded breaches might have had an influence on the proceedings' outcome grew. In 2010 this situation was observed in 15% of all the inspected cases; in 2011 in 18% of the cases, and in 2012 in 24%. As the authors of the report underline, it means that "alongside a growing number of proceedings conducted with no breaches of law, there is also a growing number of cases affected by the gravest violations" (p. 13).

9.2.1 Activity-Based Budget– central and local levels

Activity-Based Budget (ABB) is a financial plan for an entity from the public finances sector. The budget is presented in the form of a set of tasks (Misiąg 2013). In such a budget, for every task there is an indication of the unit responsible for its completion, indicators on what counts as a completed task and the resources available for its completion.

Due to its character, application of ABB allows for better assessment of the results of the administrative activities. ABB, if properly implemented, could be treated as "a government's obligation towards their citizens, an expression of intentions and objectives for whose completion the government should be held accountable" (Misiąg 2013, p. 95). The first works connected with implementation of the ABB on the central level began in 2006 and subsequent governments followed suit. Unfortunately, we observe a number of problems related to the implementation of this mechanism. They include: (a) inconsistency of legal regulations relating to ABB; as shown in an inspection of NIK (Supreme Audit Office) in 2011 the process of preparing ABB was implemented only formally; (b) unclear measures of completion of the planned tasks, which means that effectiveness of the actions cannot be verified; (c) omitting the institutions of the civil society in the implementation of ABB as training has been provided to administrative employees only.

More and more municipalities are introducing elements of ABB (Korolewska, Marchewka-Bartkowiak 2013). Examples of such places are Krakow and Poznan where ABB has been applied since 1994 and 2000, respectively. According to studies by Korolewska and Marchewka-Bartkowiak conducted in 2012 in major cities, ABB is applied in almost a quarter (23%) of the cases. Two-thirds of the cities expressed their approval for obligatory implementation of the ABB. However, a third of the cities oppose the idea of imposing the obligation to apply ABB.

One of the most serious problems related to the introduction of ABB is the fact that owing to lack of legal regulations, municipalities implement ABBs in chaotic manner. Practically speaking, it means that it is impossible to compare municipalities in terms of effectiveness of using the resources. According to the authors of the study, introducing legal regulations, as well as preparing general rules for preparing ABB, would eliminate the obstacles related to the implementation of this type of mechanism.

In conclusion, applying ABB on the local level might be an effective element of holding the local authorities accountable. However, currently there are serious obstacles connected with its implementation. Due to the lack of legal regulations and general guidelines, ABBs are implemented bottom-up, in an uncoordinated manner. Local authorities implementing these mechanisms struggle with technical and operational difficulties that they must resolve themselves.

9.3 Access to public information

9.3.1 Legal mechanisms regulating access to public information

Access to public information is guaranteed in article 61.1 of the Constitution of the Republic of Poland. In accordance with article 61.2 of the Constitution, the right to obtain information also covers access to documents and entry to sittings of collective organs of public authority formed by universal elections. Detailed regulations on access to public information are included in the bill of September 6th 2001 on access to public information (*Ustawa z dnia 6 września 2001 r. o dostępie do informacji publicznej*,

Dziennik Ustaw 2001 No. 112, item 1198). It provides the definition of public information as any information on public matters and every citizen has the right to access public information, while obtaining processed information is limited to the situation in which it is "especially vital for the public interest." The entities, which are obliged to make public information available, are public authorities and entities carrying out public tasks, as well as trade unions and political parties. The provisions specify several methods for making information public and among them the Public Information Bulletin (*Biuletyn Informacji Publicznej*, BIP) is of highest importance. It is a unified system of Internet websites where public authorities, entities performing public duties, trade unions, and political parties are obliged to post information on their functioning. Making the information public should occur without undue delay i.e. within 14 days from filing the application (according to the bill on access to public information).

9.3.2 Effectiveness of access to public information

According to DAP experts, there is a far- reaching gap between the law regulating access to public information and its daily practice. When it comes to the law, the average assessment by the experts was 7.5.

Nonetheless, the implementation of these regulations is significantly impeded, as the average rating of the experts (5.6) is only marginally above the middle point of the scale. Detailed information regarding access to public data is presented in the publication of the Klon/Jawor Association *Access to Public Data in Poland* (Gumkowska, Herbst, Kołaczyński, Kościelecka, Miazga 2013). Monitoring of Internet websites covered 15 ministerial offices and their subordinate institutions. The authors encountered significant difficulties in finding the required data on the Internet sites subject to monitoring, as on every third website there was no link to the site with data or a site map was missing. In 2/3 of cases the data could only be accessed in PDF format, which is difficult for independent analysis. The quality of data available online is also uneven. The data are presented in the form of national annual reports whereas cross-sectional studies and studies concerning smaller territorial unit are rarely published.

Another monitoring action conducted by the Klon/Jawor Association involved sending a question on public information to public institutions of different levels. 120 institutions of various kinds and various levels were monitored.

The data were most often provided by ministries and Regional Examination Boards (Okręgowa Komisja Egzaminacyjna) and least often by Local Government Appeals Court (Samorządowe Kolegium Odwoławcze): in 81% of cases no information was provided. Institutions asked for disclosure of requested data often invoked the necessity of first preparing and processing the information.

In accordance with Art.3.1 of the bill on access to public information, we can distinguish simple and processed information. Making processed (rather than simple) information public requires justification that it is of high public interest. In contacts with the institutions it was not entirely clear which data is of processed nature: it happened that some institutions would make selected information public as simple information but others treated similar or the same data as processed information. Another vague issue is the very definition of the public interest. Particular institutions interpret this term differently.

Data formats, especially PDF, often cause problems. This format is not editable and conversion of files into an editable format may pose problems to users. Researchers from the Klon/Jawor Association believe that the reason for such a frequent use of the PDF format is the fear of interference in the data, the lack of data in other formats, and the limited abilities of importing data from the databases. The latter might mean that institutions collect the data but they do not use it, do not analyze it, and do not draw conclusions from them. If this assumption is correct, it means that public institutions do not carry out analytical activities.

The above hypothesis seems to be confirmed the fact that the same type of data collected by twin institutions from different parts of the country were handed over to the researchers from the Klon/Jawor Association in a different format. In some cases the same type of data was given different names; sometimes a set of data was received in one file, in other cases in several files.

Researches from the Klon/Jawor Association point at three types of general problems connected with access to public data in Poland. First of all, quite a lot of time needs to be devoted to obtain the information. Secondly, access to public data collected by central institutions is easier than in case of local institutions. In case of central institutions, information was obtained from 10 out of 16 entities, whereas in case of local institutions from 16 out of 104 entities. A separate problem related to access to public data in Poland is the mode of operation of the Central Statistical Office (GUS). This institution charges high fees for disclosing some data, which is of public nature. The only information made public by GUS free of charge is the data posted on the Internet site or in hard copy publications, which have low circulation and allow only for basic analysis.

A different approach towards access to public data and (more generally) accountability of the Polish Parliament is presented by the authors of a report entitled *Mission Openness: Access to Information and Transparency of Activities of the Sejm of the Republic of Poland against the Objectives of the International Declaration on Opening Parliament* (Siwanowicz, Górnicki, Rzeplińska, Ścisłowska 2013). This report was prepared in cooperation with the ePanstwo Foundation and Association 61/MamPrawoWiedziec.pl and following consultations with the Civic Law Forum (Obywatelskie Forum Legislacji). The authors monitored the Internet websites of the Sejm of the Republic of Poland, of the Chancellery of the Sejm as well as an overview of existing legal acts with regard to 24 postulates of *the Declaration on Opening Parliament.* This declaration was prepared by NGOs dealing with freedom of access to public information in selected states. On the basis of data analyses its authors positively assess openness of the Sejm of the Republic of Poland. Postulates formulated by the international community of organizations for openness of parliamentary data are mostly implemented. The Polish legal system is also assessed positively. The authors conclude that it meets the expectations concerning access to public data. On the other hand, there is a problem with implementation of this law in the form of precise mechanisms used for making the parliamentary resources available.

9.4 Summary

Assessment of public responsibility and accountability of politicians is not unequivocal. Interpellations and parliamentary questions are assessed positively, whereas the substantive content of the government responses, as well as the performance of parliamentary commissions is evaluated worse which corroborates with DAP experts' opinion. Dominance of the executive over the legislative on the level of municipal authority has to be assessed negatively.

Construction, presentation, and implementation of the state budget are assessed well. Applying procedures connected with regulating public expenditure is also evaluated positively. Although there are breaches in applying procedures for public expenditure (violations of the bill on public procurement), in subsequent years the number of recorded irregularities has been decreasing. There is a problem with implementing the ABB both on the central and local level. In case of access to public information, the existing legal mechanisms can be assessed positively. A serious problem, however, is the real possibility to access this type of information.

Bibliography

Ministry of Administration and Digitization, *Budżet partycypacyjny* [Participatory Budgeting]. Available online on: https://mac.gov.pl/budzet-partycypacyjny (accessed on 04.15.2014).

CBOS 2013: *Aktualne problemy i wydarzenia* [Current Issues and Events] (278), Public Opinion Research Center, 201324.

Czy w szaleństwie jest metoda? [Is there a method in this madness?], "Kultura Liberalna."

European Social Survey Round 6: Data, Norwegian Social Science Data Services, Norway – Data Archive and distributor of ESS data, 2012.

M. Gumkowska, J. Herbst, J. Kołaczyński, K. Kościelecka, A. Miazga, *Dostęp do danych publicznych w Polsce* [Access to Public Data in Poland], Klon/Jawor Association, Warsaw 2013.

Institute of Public Affairs [online]. Available online on: http://www.isp.org.pl/petycje,740.html (accessed on 04.16.2014).

W. Kębłowski, *Budżet partycypacyjny: krótka instrukcja obsługi* [Participatory budgeting: a short user manual], Civic Institute, Warsaw 2013.

M. Korolewska, K. Marchewka-Bartkowiak, *Budżet zadaniowy w samorządach terytorialnych - analiza wyników badania ankietowego oraz studium przypadków na przykładzie miast na prawach powiatu*

[The ABB in local governments-an analysis of the results of a survey study and a case study on the example of cities with county rights], in: *Budżet Zadaniowy* [Action-based budget], edited by K. Marchewka-Bartkowiak, S. Szpringer, Studia BAS. Bureau of Research, the Chancellery of the Sejm, 2013, p. 161–188.

Leksykon budżetowy [Budgetary Lexicon]. Available online on: http://www.sejm.gov.pl/sejm7.nsf/BASLeksykon.xsp?id=667DCF4F24778F74C1257A710030C2E9&litera=B (accessed on 04.15.2014).

W. Misiąg, *Siedem lat wdrażania budżetu zadaniowego – refleksje i prognozy*, w: *Budżet Zadaniowy* [7 years of implementing ABB-reflections and forecast], in: *Budżet Zadaniowy* [Activity-based budget], edited by K. Marchewka-Bartkowiak, S. Szpringer, Studia BAS. Bureau of Research, the Chancellery of the Sejm, 2013, p. 85–102.

Dyktat czy uczestnictwo?: diagnoza partycypacji publicznej w Polsce [Dictate or Participation?: a diagnosis of public participation in Poland], edited by A. Olech, Institute of Public Affairs, Warsaw 2012.

Opening Parliament. Available online on: http://www.openingparliament.org/ (accessed on 09.23.2013).

P. Pomianowski, P. Golędzinowski, T. Lewiński, *Raport z monitoringu aktywności biur poselskich oraz efektywności wydawanych na nie środków publicznych* [A report on monitoring of activities of constituency offices as well as effectiveness of public resources spent on these offices], 2011.

"Stocznia" association, *Raport końcowy z badania efektywności mechanizmów konsultacji społecznych* [A final report on a study of effectiveness of mechanisms of public consultations], SMG/KRC Poland Media S.A. 2011.

Senate of the Republic of Poland, *W Senacie o prawie do petycji* [In the senate on the right to petition]. Available online on: http://www.senat.gov.pl/aktualnosci/art,550,w-senacie-o-prawie-do-petycji.html (accessed on 04.16.2014).

M. Siwanowicz, J. Górnicki, M. Rzeplińska, A. Ścisłowska, *Misja Otwartość: Dostęp do informacji i transparentność Działań Sejmu RP na tle założeń międzynarodowej Deklaracji w sprawie otwartości parlamentu* [Mission Openness: Access to information and transparency of Activities of the Sejm of the Republic of Poland against the objectives of the international Declaration on opening Parliament], ePaństwo Foundation, Association 61/MamPrawoWiedzieć.pl, Warsaw 2013.

Public Procurement Office, *Wyniki przeprowadzonych w 2012 r. przez Prezesa Urzędu Zamówien Publicznych kontroli zamówień współfinansowanych ze środków Unii Europejskiej* [Results of control of procurement co-financed by the EU conducted by the President of the Public Procurement Office in 2012], 2013.

Ustawa o dostępie do informacji publicznej [The bill on access to public information], Non-Governmental Centre on Access to Public Information. Available online on: http://informacjapubliczna.org.pl/31,265,ustawa_o_dostepie_do_informacji_publicznej.html (accessed on 02.03.2014).

M. Zubik, *Funkcja kontrolna Sejmu* [Control Function of the Sejm], 2001.

10. Responsiveness of politicians

Appropriate reaction to citizens' expectations, needs and demands, i.e. authority responsiveness, include a wide range of mechanisms and practices both within institutions and in relations of state institutions with citizens. The translation of public preferences into politics is not a simple task: on the one hand, the authorities must take into account citizens' expectations; on the other hand, however, representative democracy assumes a selection of competent elites whose task is to form these expectations into coherent and feasible policy. In this chapter the issue of authority responsiveness is discussed in three aspects. They include: (1) procedures of public consultation; (2) availability of MPs and local authorities to citizens and (3) assessment of authority responsiveness by citizens.

10.1 Procedures of public consultation

The first area comprises procedures of public consultation. In this report we define them as "an organized methods of obtaining opinions and views from entities (individuals and institutions) who are going to be indirectly or directly affected by the results of actions proposed by the administration" ("Stocznia" association 2011, p. 9). Our analysis starts from presenting legal mechanisms regulating procedures of public consultation.

DAP experts were asked for assessment of public consultations conducted by the central and local authority. The experts were rather negative when assessing consultations conducted by the central authority. The average rating was 5, which means that "only issues in which consultations are obligatory are consulted," indicating moderate openness of the central authority towards conducting public consultation. Assessment is even more negative when it comes to the real impact of consultations on the authority decisions. This aspect gained the average value of 4.2.

Assessment of consultations conducted by the local authority is slightly better. From the experts' opinions we can infer that consultations sometimes cover the issues, which are not obligatory. The average assessment of the scope of issues subjected to consultations was 5.2. Assessment of the real impact of public consultations conducted by the local authority on their decisions was rated at 5.4.

The data on using procedures of public consultation in Polish municipalities are presented in a publication entitled *Dictate or Participation? A diagnosis of political participation in Poland*, prepared by the Institute of Public Affairs, edited by Anna Olech (2012). The publication is based on representative sample of municipal offices and adult population of Poland. The authors state that the authorities of 80% of Polish municipalities consult the provisions of the budget bill. It means that in the remaining 20% of cases budget bills are not consulted, is spite of the fact that such consultations are required by law. In case of 93% of Polish municipalities the authorities informed their inhabitants about the mechanisms adopted in the budget bill and in other bills. Only occasionally were the provisions of adopted bills justified and explained. Organizing meetings by the municipality authority is a popular form of contacting local inhabitants.

A study of quality and effectiveness of public consultation was also conducted by the "Stocznia" association in cooperation with SMG/KRC Poland Media (2011). This research was fielded in 2010 and included 515 offices. This study resulted in creation of two indexes of public consultations. One of them concerns the quality and effectiveness of consultations in public institutions; the other is about the quality of consultations of particular documents. The indices are based on 51 indicators from 3 data sources.

The result is the average of standardized sub-indices, which takes values from 0 to 100. Index values need to be treated as general assessment of particular dimensions of public consultations on a scale from 0 to 100 points, the higher the value the better the assessment. The index of quality and effectiveness of consultation in offices assesses the following issues: willingness to conduct consultations, preparation for conducting them, and the degree to which institutions meet fundamental standards connected with conducting public consultations. It is based on three dimensions: procedures, practice, and perception. The procedural dimension checks whether specific procedures comprising public consultations are applied in a given institution. The dimension of practice answers the question to what degree and how these procedures are met. The third dimension concerns the perception of consultations, i.e. how they are assessed by their participants.

When comparing the assessment of particular dimensions, the perception of consultation was assessed the highest (the average score was 68 points); the practice of consultations was assessed slightly worse; and the procedures were evaluated worst. The hierarchy of assessment of particular aspects of consultations is the same regardless of the type of institution.

The average result in all the 3 dimensions for all institutions covered by the research was 51.8 points, which means that the ideal model of public consultations is met halfway. According to the researches, this result is far from satisfactory.

The second index created by the "Stocznia" association and SMG/KRC examined the quality of consultations of particular documents. In calculations of this index, a unit of analysis was an individual document prepared by an institution. These analyses included 714 documents prepared in 578 offices. Following types of documents were analyzed: development strategy, strategy for resolving social problems, the study of land use planning and development, the natural environment protection program, the program of public schools, the program of cooperation with NGOs, and the budget. The type of documents that was assessed best turned out to be development strategies, whose average result was 67 points. Social consultations concerning natural environment protection programs were assessed worst, as the average result was 58 points.

When documents are compared with regard to 3 dimensions of the index (procedures, practice and perception), 2 groups can be distinguished: some are assessed better in terms of procedures, while others in terms of perception. Consultations on development strategies, the strategy for resolving social problems, as well as consultations on schools received relatively high assessment in terms of procedures. According to the authors of the report, it results from the fact that these types of projects are deeply rooted in the Polish local government practice. The other reasons are: public interest and well defined target groups. These types of documents are, at the same time, assessed lowest in terms of perception. The second group of documents comprise programs of cooperation with NGOs and natural environment programs. Consultations of the documents are quite well perceived but compliance with appropriate procedures is much worse. Consultations of these two types of documents are also worst assessed in terms of practice, hence the low quality of the consultation process.

10.2 Availability of MPs, councillors, town and city mayors for contact with citizens

10.2.1 Legal framework of contacts between MPs and citizens

The institution, which ensures communication between parliamentarians and citizens, is the constituency office. Its legal status is regulated by the bill on implementation of the mandate of Members of Parliament (*Ustawa z dnia 9 maja 1996 r. o wykonaniu mandatu posła i senatora*, Dziennik Ustaw 2011 No.7, item 29). According to article 23 of the bill, the Members of Parliament (both the Sejm and Senate) establish constituency offices (individually or in cooperation with other MPs) in order to perform their operations at field level. These resources cannot be used for financing of, among others, political parties, social organizations or foundations. The funds are at the disposal of MPs, and every year they are obliged to submit a report to the Chancellery of the Sejm on spending the funds allocated for their constituency offices.

10.2.2 Contact channels between MPs and citizens

DAP experts differ in their opinions on the performance of constituency offices; the average grade is close to the middle point of this scale but with a substantial standard deviation, which means that individual expert opinions are often far above or below the average.

Fig./Tab. 10.1: Assessment of performance of constituency offices

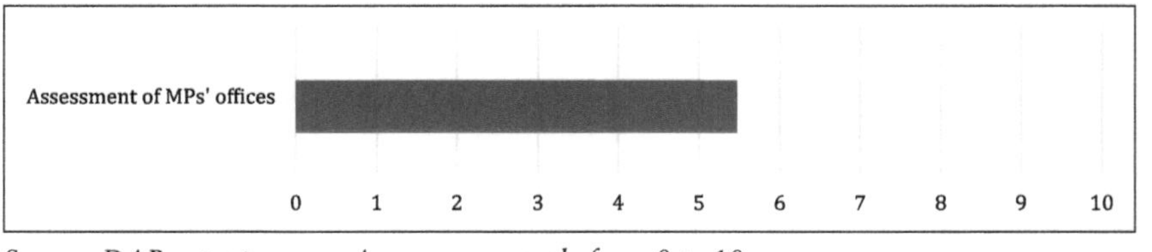

Source: DAP expert survey. Average on a scale from 0 to 10

A detailed study of the performance of constituency offices is included in *Report on Monitoring of Activity in Constituency Offices and Effectiveness of Public Funds Allocated to Them* prepared by the Association of Students, Graduates, and Friends of the College of Interdepartmental Studies in the Humanities at the University of Warsaw "ProCollegio" (Pomianowski, Golędzinowski and Lewiński, 2011). Research activities were conducted between March and September 2011. The study involved 3 telephone attempts to reach constituency offices of all MPs. In case of 73% of offices 2 or 3 attempts were successful, which authors of the study regarded as a satisfactory result. In case of 19% of constituency offices only one attempt was successful, whereas in the remaining 8% of constituency offices none of the 3 attempts was successful. This means that in case of over a quarter (27%) of constituency offices there are serious problems regarding the public availability of these offices. Additionally, every constituency office was sent an e-mail containing two questions: on the progress of legislative works on an indicated issue, and on a selected legal problem. The questions were asked independently. The first question was answered by 108 offices (which constitute 28% of constituency offices with an Internet website); the second question was answered by 153 offices (40% of offices with an Internet website). This result is obviously unsatisfactory.

An important contact channel between MPs and the electorate are the Internet websites of MPs. The "ProCollegio" research showed that 17% of MPs have no website pages. The content of websites of MPs was assessed negatively. Only in case of 52% of parliamentarians running their websites (who constitute 43% of all MPs) the page contained information on opening hours of the office. Only every third website (i.e. 28% of all MPs) provided the name of at least 1 person working in the office. Little more than 3/4 of the websites (77% of the websites, 65% of MPs) contained the MP's CV. Linking the website to the Internet resources of the Sejm was also assessed negatively.

A separate module in this study of constituency offices was a questionnaire for individual completion containing questions on the office operation. It could be filled both in hard and soft copy. As few as 72 constituency offices provided the answers, which constitutes 16% of the total. Authors of the report believe that the result shows that "the vast majority of constituency offices ignore citizens' right of access to public information."

On the basis of the data obtained from those constituency offices that provided the answers we may attempt to build their profile. The average constituency office is open for 33 hours per week. Most of the MPs' meetings take place regularly, usually on Mondays. Some MPs were able to schedule a meeting on another day. Only 19% of constituency offices are located in buildings adapted to the needs of the disabled. Employees of 14% of offices admitted that information on the operation of the constituency office and MP's co-workers on the Sejm website was outdated.

In accordance with the bill on implementation of the mandate of Members of Parliament, MPs have a right to intervene in activities of government administrative body, a local authority, a state-owned enterprise, and a social organization, as well as in non-state economic units. Authors of the report asked office employees about the number of interventions in different types of institutions. MPs most often intervened in the activities of government administrative bodies, slightly less often in local authorities. Interventions rarely took place in state-owned or municipal enterprises, social or professional organizations, and private companies. In conclusion, the study shows that constituency offices are not properly organized.

10.2.3 Contact channels of local government with citizens

In the work *Dictate or Participation?* (Olech 2012) the authors study the availability of the local authorities for citizens. The possibility to contact the local executive is commonly available. Only in case of 5% of Polish municipalities the mayors and their deputies have no regular office hours indicating their availability for contact. As far as the councils are concerned, in 11% of municipalities all councillors have regular office hours, while in 20% of municipalities some councillors have office hours.

10.3 Citizen assessment of authority responsiveness

Social reception of public consultations conducted by the authorities is presented in a study of CBOS Public Opinion Research Centre (2013). It shows a rather negative picture. Only slightly more than a quarter of Poles (28%) believed that important state-related decisions were consulted with the society. Almost 2/3 of respondents (62%) indicated unsatisfactory level of consultations. The results were similar on the issue of whether, when taking decisions, the authorities take into account citizens' views. Only 24% of respondents replied in the affirmative. Almost 2/3 of the respondents (64%) stated that the authorities did not pay any attention to their views.

In the international comparative study called European Social Survey (*ESS Round* 6 2012), respondents from Poland and other European countries were asked to evaluate the level of authority responsiveness. In the social perception, Polish authorities do not explain their decisions to citizens as often as authorities of the mature European democracies (the average response was 3.64 for Poland versus 4.95 for mature democracies of Western Europe). However, it needs to be noted that Poles give better ratings of this aspect of democracy than inhabitants of other countries of Central and Eastern Europe (the average for Poland was 3.64 versus 3.56 for countries of Central and Eastern Europe).

10.4 Participatory budgets

A recent positive development in terms of authority responsiveness on the local level is the spread of participatory budgeting by city and municipality authorities. Participatory budgeting means "a decision-making process in which community members contribute to creating a city's budget and, at the same time, decide on allocation of a certain part of public resources" (Kębłowski 2013, p. 8). Participatory budgeting includes a discussion among community members, which concerns clearly defined and limited financial resources, where at least one of the discussed expenses involves the whole municipality. In addition to this, the results of the participatory budgeting process should be binding and it should be a long-term process (not a one-off event).

In terms of authority responsiveness, the following features of participatory budgeting are vital (as in Kębłowski 2013): It …

- allows one to get detailed information from community members on the performance of municipal authorities;
- bridges the distance between the authority and citizens;
- builds trust of citizens to the local government and its representatives;
- serves democratization and the decision-making process;
- increases the transparency in handling public resources in a municipality;
- allows one to initiate a dialogue between officials and NGOs.

This last aspect is especially vital as NGOs are grass-roots initiatives, which often draw our attention to "neglected problems of cities and propose alternative mechanisms of their management" (p. 15).

In Poland, participatory budgeting was first applied in Sopot in 2011. In total, approximately 80 Polish local governments have conducted or are planning to carry out the first trials for introduction of participatory budgeting *(Is There a Method in This Madness?)*. The idea of applying participatory budgeting was backed by the central authority: the term "participatory budget" was included in the Budgetary Lexicon of the Sejm *(Budgetary Lexicon)*. Information on participatory budgeting was also posted on the main website of the Ministry of Administration and Digitalization *(Participatory Budgeting | Ministry of Administration and Digitization)*.

Increasingly frequent application of participatory budgeting is undoubtedly a positive phenomenon. However, the methodology of preparing and implementing participatory budgeting raises a few concerns. When analyzing the first participatory budgets in Sopot, carried out in 2011 and 2012, Kębłowski (2013) indicates a number of problems connected with correct implementation of this procedure. One of them is very low turnout during the meetings with community members. According to the author, it may be caused by unattractive and inefficient information campaign. Another problem concerns the role of community members in the procedure of preparing participatory budget. During the first phase of works, community members' activity is narrowed down to presenting their proposals for allocation of funds on a form previously prepared by the city authority. During the next phase, followed by preliminary formal and legal selection of the submitted projects, community members select projects to be implemented by popular vote.

Community members neither participate in the selection of applications nor monitor an implementation of the accepted projects. The procedure of implementation of participatory budgets is prepared in such a way as "not to be too demanding for the participants" (Kębłowski 2013, p. 34).

Introduction of participatory budgeting does not lead to a discussion on urban policy. Neither does it have an educational function for community members, since they "are not treated as equal partners in the public debate, as people who are equally responsible for the city" (p. 34). It should be noted, however, that a range of investments submitted for participatory budgeting have already been implemented in Sopot, while others are currently being implemented. Participatory budget is undoubtedly a valuable initiative and it is positive that it is being applied more and more often. The aspect that requires improvement is the method of its implementation.

10.5 Right to petition

A key problem related to authority responsiveness is lack of a bill regulating the citizens' right to submit petitions. Experts in this matter are unanimous in their opinion that petitions are an important instrument of direct democracy (the voice of Senator Mieczysław Augustyn during a seminar dedicated to regulating the right to petition, *In the Senate on the right to petition*). The Ombudsman Irena Lipowicz (during the same seminar) pointed out that in case of crisis of social confidence in public institutions, it is the petition that might give the citizens a feeling that they have an influence on the decision-making process.

In turn Tomasz Schimanek noted that petitions might be a method for overcoming citizens' passivity. Lack of a proper bill is even more symptomatic as Art.63 of the Constitution of the Republic of Poland guarantees this right to citizens. During the 2007-2011 term, the Senate prepared a draft of the bill, which was then submitted to the Sejm, but the Sejm did not have enough time to vote on the bill by the end of the term. During the current term of the Parliament, work on the bill regulating the right to petition has begun again.

10.6 Summary

One of the main mechanisms facilitating authority responsiveness is public consultation. Consultations conducted by the central authority are assessed negatively. DAP experts agreed that only obligatory matters are consulted. Real impact of consultations on authority decisions is assessed even worse, while consultations carried out by local authority can be evaluated slightly better. They received higher notes both when it comes to their scope and the impact they had on the authority decisions. In a detailed study of various aspects of public consultations in different types of institutions ("Stocznia" association and SMG/KRC), averaged assessment of consultations was 52 points out of 100. It means that 50% of the criteria of well-conducted public consultations were met. This result is disappointing.

Assessment of MPs' contact with citizens cannot be regarded as satisfactory either. In a study of availability of MPs (carried out by "ProCollegio") it turned out that, in case of a high number of constituency offices, citizens may have difficulties in contacting their parliamentarians. There are even problems with establishing office hours during which MPs are available. Nevertheless, in case of representatives of the local authority, the possibility of contact between a citizen and the authority does not raise major objections.

The negative picture of authority responsiveness is reinforced by citizens' opinions. The vast majority of respondents in a CBOS study believe that significant decisions are not consulted with community members and the authorities do not take into account citizens' preferences. It might be reassuring that, in the study by ESS, Poland scores better than the average for countries of Central and Eastern Europe in social perception of authority responsiveness. However, inhabitants of Western European countries assess their authority responsiveness much better than Poles.

A positive phenomenon, which impacts responsiveness of the local authorities, is the increasingly frequent application of participatory budgeting by municipalities. So far, 80 municipalities have implemented or are planning to implement such mechanisms. In numerous places investment proposals submitted in the process of participatory budgeting have been executed. Lack of a bill regulating the citizens' right to petition must be assessed negatively. The absence of proper legislation is a significant hindrance to the full exercise of this right.

Bibliography

Ministry of Administration and Digitization, *Budżet partycypacyjny* [Participatory Budgeting]. Available online on: https://mac.gov.pl/budzet-partycypacyjny (accessed on 04.15.2014).

CBOS 2013: *Aktualne problemy i wydarzenia* [Current Issues and Events] (278), Public Opinion Research Center, 201324.

Czy w szaleństwie jest metoda? [Is there a method in this madness?], "Kultura Liberalna."

European Social Survey Round 6: Data, Norwegian Social Science Data Services, Norway – Data Archive and distributor of ESS data, 2012.

M. Gumkowska, J. Herbst, J. Kołaczyński, K. Kościelecka, A. Miazga, *Dostęp do danych publicznych w Polsce* [Access to Public Data in Poland], the Klon/Jawor Association, Warsaw 2013.

Institute of Public Affairs [online]. Available online on: http://www.isp.org.pl/petycje,740.html (accessed on 04.16.2014).

W. Kębłowski, *Budżet partycypacyjny: krótka instrukcja obsługi* [Participatory budgeting: a short user manual], the Civic Institute, Warsaw 2013.

M. Korolewska, K. Marchewka-Bartkowiak, *Budżet zadaniowy w samorządach terytorialnych - analiza wyników badania ankietowego oraz studium przypadków na przykładzie miast na prawach powiatu* [The ABB in local governments-an analysis of the results of a survey study and a case study on the example of cities with county rights], in: *Budżet Zadaniowy* [Action-based budget], edited by K. Marchewka-Bartkowiak, S. Szpringer, BAS Studies, the Bureau of Research, the Chancellery of the Sejm, 2013, p. 161–188.

Leksykon budżetowy [Budgetary Lexicon]. Available online on: http://www.sejm.gov.pl/sejm7.nsf/BASLeksykon.xsp?id=667DCF4F24778F74C1257A710030C2E9&litera=B (accessed on 04.15.2014).

W. Misiąg, *Siedem lat wdrażania budżetu zadaniowego – refleksje i prognozy*, w: *Budżet Zadaniowy* [7 years of implementing ABB-reflections and forecast], in: *Budżet Zadaniowy* [Action-based budget], edited by K. Marchewka-Bartkowiak, S. Szpringer, BAS Studies, the Bureau of Research, the Chancellery of the Sejm, 2013, p. 85–102.

Dyktat czy uczestnictwo? : diagnoza partycypacji publicznej w Polsce [Dictate or Participation?: a diagnosis of public participation in Poland], edited by A. Olech, t. 1, Institute of Public Affairs, Warsaw 2012.

Opening Parliament. Available online on: http://www.openingparliament.org/ (accessed on 09.23.2013).

P. Pomianowski, P. Golędzinowski, T. Lewiński, *Raport z monitoringu aktywności biur poselskich oraz efektywności wydawanych na nie środków publicznych* [A report on monitoring of activities of constituency offices as well as effectiveness of public resources spent on these offices], 2011.

"Stocznia" association, *Raport końcowy z badania efektywności mechanizmów konsultacji społecznych* [A final report on a study of effectiveness of mechanisms of public consultations], SMG/KRC Poland Media S.A. 2011.

Senate of the Republic of Poland, *W Senacie o prawie do petycji* [In the senate on the right to petition]. Available online on: http://www.senat.gov.pl/aktualnosci/art,550,w-senacie-o-prawie-do-petycji.html (accessed on 04.16.2014).

M. Siwanowicz, J. Górnicki, M. Rzeplińska, A. Ścisłowska, *Misja Otwartość: Dostęp do informacji i transparentność Działań Sejmu RP na tle założeń międzynarodowej Deklaracji w sprawie otwartości parlamentu* [Mission Openness: Access to information and transparency of Activities of the Sejm of the Republic of Poland against the objectives of the international Declaration on opening Parliament], ePaństwo Foundation, Association 61/MamPrawoWiedzieć.pl, Warsaw 2013.

Public Procurement Office, *Wyniki przeprowadzonych w 2012 r. przez Prezesa Urzędu Zamówien Publicznych kontroli zamówień współfinansowanych ze środków Unii Europejskiej* [Results of control of procurement co-financed by the EU conducted by the President of the Public Procurement Office in 2012], 2013.

Ustawa o dostępie do informacji publicznej [The bill on access to public information], Non-Governmental Centre on Access to Public Information. Available online on: http://informacjapubliczna.org.pl/31,265,ustawa_o_dostepie_do_informacji_publicznej.html (accessed on 02.03.2014).

M. Zubik, *Funkcja kontrolna Sejmu* [Control Function of the Sejm], 2001.

Summary

The state of Polish democracy of 2012–2013 is assessed as satisfactory, or even good, especially when analysed against Central Europe. In this respect the results of our audit are in accordance with numerous international projects assessing similar issues when the same period of time is considered, namely *Freedom House Ranking*, *Bertelsmann Transformative Index* and *Rule of Law Index*. Using the sport metaphor it might be stated that in all of these rankings the Polish democracy makes it "to the medals", as it usually occupies the honourable second or third place behind the safe leader, which is Estonia. In fact, however, the place itself is less important than the dynamics of changes in time; even at the beginning of the current millennium Poland was behind the leaders of the region in many aspects.

Our initiative to study the state of Polish democracy every 2 years is an endeavour complementary to the abovementioned projects. It differs from them in that it is a more detailed analysis. Unlike those projects, ours is not only a comparative attempt. For that reason we make use in our audit of international comparisons. It is especially important in the first "pilot" edition of the Democratic Audit of Poland. In the future our project is to become a permanent element of the Polish public scene. Over the years our analysis will be diachronically comparable as the subsequent reports will refer to this benchmark audit.Due to the fact that this study is opening the whole series, we had no possibility to conduct comparative longitudinal comparisons. Therefore, a high number of our analyses are shown against different types of obtainable data from the past. While preparing this "pilot" report we decided that synchronic comparisons to other countries of the regions would be useful as well.

The time has come for several general conclusions. In this part we also make an overall assessment of a given area, taking into consideration all the aspects, on a scale from "0" to "10" where the latter means the state of ideal democracy in a given area. In some cases of substantial differences in assessing particular aspects we make use of a value range, e.g. 7-8 or even (when the discrepancy is even greater) 5-7, as in the case of the rule of law. It must be added that this assessment is realistic in the sense that we are trying to assess Polish democracy from the perspective of what is feasible in a young democracy and the main reference points are the countries of the former "Eastern block," and more precisely those of Central Eastern Europe.

Contemporary Polish democracy can rarely be found at fault in terms of civil rights scope and practical application. There is Polish political community and the rights of Polish citizens are respected to a satisfactory degree. However, there are problems with representation of selected minority groups and individuals not being Polish citizens but permanently resident in the country. On a more optimistic note, the Polish society is tolerant towards newcomers from abroad, regardless of their formal status, and open in terms of greater inclusion.

Overall assessment: 8

Polish democracy assessment in terms of the quality of the rule of law is ambiguous. It seems that, similarly to some other aspects, formal systemic solutions may be evaluated higher than the practice of functioning of the institutions. The judiciary is well funded and has adequate level of human resources; however, they are often not used effectively. Serious problems are: low level of legal culture in the society as well as an inefficient functioning of the judiciary. Democracy is weakened by low quality of law-making, its massive inflation, as well as courts' slowness to act.

Overall assessment: 5-7

The media in Poland are free and ensure access to information concerning the public sphere, but the level and objectivity of the news might in some cases raise some doubts. The problems of the mass media in Poland resemble those in other countries of Central Europe and in the most developed countries as well. These include: economic weakness of the printed media, de-professionalization of the journalists, and tabloidization of information. Public media are being weakened by politicisation, whereas private media by economic dependency. Nonetheless, against the media in other countries of the region Polish media seem to be more immune both to the influences of high-finance as well as direct "political parallelism." Their relative independence and significant pluralism are also related to the size of the country.

Overall assessment: 6

Opinions are divided on the question of corruption in Poland. Public opinion believes this phenomenon is a serious problem, especially in the public sphere. It is also believed that the country lacks political will to combat corruption and the undertaken activities are insufficient. At the same time, international organizations dealing with global corruption assessment place Poland among countries relatively free from the risk of corruption. According to them, it is lobbying that causes problems, as due to imperfect laws this phenomenon is not subject to sufficient control. Whilst it seems that we have tackled the most obvious corruption signs on the government and ministry level, the phenomena of corruption, nepotism, and patronage still seem to be present on the local level.

Overall assessment: 7

Most citizens of Poland believe democracy is the best possible system (however, it is surprising that a relatively big group of citizens would approve of the authoritarian rule) but the performance of democracy in Poland is assessed in rather negative terms as Poles believe that democratic institutions (Polish Sejm and Senate) function badly, the key democracy functions are not fulfilled (it especially concerns economic and redistributive functions of the state, important to recognise the state as democratic). This belief is followed by a low level of social capital: lack of trust in democratic institutions, lack of sense of political agency both on the national and local level, as well as a low level of public participation. In short: democracy foundations in Poland are stable, whereas the assessment of its everyday functionality and specific institutions is subject to considerable fluctuations dependent on the economic situation and the political climate. The same situation is taking place in all young democracies.

Overall assessment: 7

Public administration in Poland is top-heavy and relatively costly. Unfortunately, this does not translate into its efficiency. Other concerns include its rationality (public offices are at risk of politicisation, procedures are complex and lengthy, and unprofessional officials are not liable for the decisions taken). Despite finding irregularities, NIK (Supreme Audit Office) relatively well assesses carrying out particular national functions by the administration. Its final assessment is not unequivocally positive, though. Many aspects have improved in recent years but, according to Poles, the reality of public offices has changed only slightly. At the same time it is worth mentioning that in recent years a number of innovations have been introduced into the system of public administration. Currently it is more open to the citizen participation. The law-making process, while far from ideal, remains under control of social organizations.

Overall assessment: 5-7

Political process in Poland is conducted in accordance with the democratic norms and the citizens exercise their rights freely. The most important institution of modern democracy, namely electoral representation, is well organised and there is every reason to assess this aspect of Polish democracy as close to ideal. International agencies share this opinion when evaluating this aspect of Polish democracy. Obviously, it does not mean that when having a closer look we will not see some room for improvement of the status quo. We see them and point at them mainly in relation to the technical and logistic procedures of elections where substantial improvements would be welcome. This process requires wise legislation and will of responsible citizens to support politicians there. Putting aside ideological emotions, in the future more consideration should be given to non-representation, the situation of disadvantaged groups, and political influence of groups, which have been kept away from the decision-making process.

Overall assessment: 9

Polish political parties and the party system have become more mature and consolidated in recent years. The structural overview of the changes in the Polish party system points at a similarity to the party systems of long-term democracies. It is characterised by more stability and predictability, lasting coalitions and blocks competing against one another. A weak link of the party system operation is still its low legitimacy in the eyes of citizens who are reluctant to identify with the parties, as they believe they are not effective enough when representing them. The Polish system is not "frozen" and thanks to the reasonable proportional electoral law citizens can successfully create new political parties, should the need arise. At the same time citizens do not quite understand how the electoral law works, which might be attributed to the presence of numerous ideologically excited "experts" trying to convince them that the electoral law leads to high partisanship of Polish politics. A high level of political apathy of Poles and a lack of trust in public institutions is also worrying. Numerous faults of the system of financing political parties also constitute problems that call for consideration and reasonable solution.

<u>Overall assessment: 7</u>

In this audit we assess and discuss the issues of <u>accountability of politicians</u>. Practical use of interpellations and parliamentary questions by MPs can be positively assessed. The situation is much worse, however, when it comes to the government's response. Activities of parliamentary commissions are also criticised. There are irregularities in procedures for public tenders (violations of the bill on public procurement), although in the subsequent years the number of recorded irregularities is decreasing. Real access to public information is still a significant problem, despite numerous innovations in this area.

We have noted negative evaluation of the public consultation conducted by the central authorities. According to experts, the only issues subject to the public consultation process are the obligatory ones and the public consultation has limited impact on the decisions of the authorities. The public consultations conducted by the local authorities are slightly better but also critically assessed. In the detailed assessment of various aspects of the public consultation process (conducted by sociological institutes "Stocznia" and SMG/KRC) the average assessment of public consultation was 52 out of 100 points, which means that the analysed cases displayed only half of the features of the well-conducted processes of this type.

Overall assessment: 6-7

Communication between MPs and their electorate could also improve. Currently, voters sometimes have problems when trying to get in touch with their parliamentary representatives. The situation is slightly better when it comes to contacting the local authorities.

A negative picture of the authorities' responsiveness is supplemented by the assessment of citizens. The vast majority of the CBOS (Public Opinion Research Centre) respondents believe that important decisions are not consulted with the inhabitants. Moreover, the authorities, when taking decisions, fail to take into consideration their opinions. It might be reassuring that in the light of the research by ESS the social reception of the authorities' responsiveness in Poland is better than an average assessment in the countries of Central and Eastern Europe. At the same time, it must be noted that when it comes to many issues citizens fail to make an effort; they do not devote necessary energy or enough time to become fully acquainted with the essence of the problem they are so critical about. Authorities' responsiveness makes sense only when it addresses the needs of a competent and responsible citizen.

Overall assessment: 7

In conclusion it must be stressed that Polish democracy at the beginning of this second decade of the 21st century is assessed quite well. Such evaluation is obviously always relative so it should be stated that our democracy looks quite well in relation to its state several years back and favourably against the countries from the region of similar history and similar level of development. However, we are far from the quality of democracy noted for instance in Scandinavia. Numerous detailed, technical aspects of our democracy require urgent intervention. We elaborate on them in the corresponding chapters.

Warsaw Studies in Politics and Society

Edited by Radosław Markowski

Vol. 1 Izabela Handzlik / Łukasz Sorokowski (eds.): Found in Multiculturalism. Acceptance or Challenge? 2014.

Vol. 2 Radosław Markowski / Michał Kotnarowski / Michał Wenzel / Marta Żerkowska-Balas: Democratic Audit of Poland 2014. 2015.

www.peterlang.com

www.ingramcontent.com/pod-product-compliance
Ingram Content Group UK Ltd.
Pitfield, Milton Keynes, MK11 3LW, UK
UKHW041829100926
8556IPUK00002B/83

9 783631 656914